VIETNAM: REMEMBRANCES OF A NATIVE AMERICAN SOLDIER

VIETNAM

REMEMBRANCES OF

A NATIVE AMERICAN SOLDIER

RON C. WOOD

iUniverse, Inc.
Bloomington

Vietnam:
Remembrances of a Native American Soldier

iUniverse books may be ordered through booksellers or by contacting:

iUniverse
1663 Liberty Drive
Bloomington, IN 47403
www.iuniverse.com
1-800-Authors (1-800-288-4677)

Because of the dynamic nature of the Internet, any web addresses or links contained in this book may have changed since publication and may no longer be valid. The views expressed in this work are solely those of the author and do not necessarily reflect the views of the publisher, and the publisher hereby disclaims any responsibility for them.

Any people depicted in stock imagery provided by Thinkstock are models, and such images are being used for illustrative purposes only.

Certain stock imagery © Thinkstock.

ISBN: 978-1-4620-1585-6 (sc)
ISBN: 978-1-4620-1586-3 (e)

Printed in the United States of America

iUniverse rev. date: 08/09/2011

CONTENTS

PREFACE

I returned from Vietnam in April of 1968 and immediately found a job for the summer and then re-enrolled in college in the fall. I did not give my Vietnam experience much thought but considered my experience as something that I had done which was now history and I put it behind me and moved forward with my life. Other than some minor gastrointestinal problems and a short stay in the Prescott VA hospital, I did not feel traumatized or "messed up" by my Vietnam experiences. I worked summers and attended school fulltime in the winters and graduated from college in1972 after getting married in 1971.

For about 15 years, I forgot about Vietnam and had little curiosity about it and focused on school, marriage, family, and career. In the early 1980s, I began to read books by fellow veterans of the Vietnam war and came to realize that every single veteran had a different war experience dependent upon his/her branch of service, location in Vietnam, or time period during his/her tour of duty. I read dozens of books about Vietnam but only two were similar to the experience I had in the southern Mekong delta region of South Vietnam in the time period of late 1966 to early 1968. The factors that made my experience different was that I was stationed on an eight man advisory team in a former Specials Forces A team camp. We lived with and interacted with Vietnamese civilians and soldiers on a daily basis. There were very few conventional US Army troops in the Mekong delta and it was a war being fought half heartedly by Vietnamese soldiers. I was a Native American and other than my height, I looked like and could relate to the brown skinned Vietnamese people on a very personal level.

For these reasons and the fact that I have gained an appreciation for history and the passing on of knowledge and experience from one generation to the next, I wanted to leave a written record of my experience for my children and posterity. I came to realize that my Vietnam experience had a greater impact on me than I had realized and I wanted to share with my children and grandchildren, some of my experiences so that they might better understand me. I also wanted them to appreciate more fully the many wonderful benefits they have living in a free country like America and being relatively safe most of their lives.

This book is therefore dedicated to my children,
Lisa, Craig, Dawn and Shandiin

and my grandchildren
Violet, Kevin, Trevor, Stellane, Brayden, Naatani
and Nizhoni and those yet to arrive

I want to thank my wife, Genevieve Jackson, who did much of the typing and gave technical and supportive assistance throughout. I also want to thank several of my friends that provided valuable input and fresh perspectives on the manuscript.

Out of respect for the privacy of my former team members and Vietnamese acquaintances, I have elected to change the names of persons mentioned in this book.

CHAPTER 1

IN THE ARMY NOW

I woke up, face down on the smooth, cool, concrete floor of a jail cell. Looking at the gray steel bars, and the lime green walls of my cell, I knew where I was. I had been here before. At nineteen years old, this was my fourth incarceration for illegal alcohol consumption and I knew that I could not continue living my life like this without developing a serious alcohol abuse problem. I made my one phone call to a buddy who bailed me out of jail. Later that same day, I made a decision to drastically change my life. My philosophy at that time was to work hard and play hard. I did well in school and studied from Monday to Friday but on weekends, I considered that my time to play. Unfortunately, alcohol was a big part of my social life and in an urban area, getting caught was inevitable. Upon release from jail, I went directly to the US Army recruiter's office and volunteered for military service.

I was raised on two Indian reservations in Arizona, the Colorado River Indian Reservation in southwest Arizona and the Navajo Reservation in Tuba City and Fort Defiance in northeast Arizona. During my last two years of high school, my family moved off reservation to Flagstaff, Arizona, where I discovered that I was a minority and there was racism in reservation border towns. That was my main excuse for my underage drinking but I did well academically in school. I vaguely remember references to Vietnam in 1962 on the news stations but was not concerned about it. I remember a *Life* magazine article that had pictures of American troops in combat in Vietnam. I remember telling my siblings that if I ever had to go into the military, I would want to go to a unit that actually saw combat action. Little did I realize that within four years, I would be living my boast. By my senior year in high school in 1963-4, I was very aware of Vietnam and upon entering college I became aware of the draft and lottery system.

My mother passed away during my freshman year at Arizona State University and I returned home in my sophomore year to help my dad raise my younger brother and sister. I could not get along with my father at that time. After one semester at NAU, I decided to transfer back to ASU, but my local draft board told me not to bother trying to get back into school at ASU since I would get drafted first. The final straw occurred for me when I finished my last test exam of the semester and decided to party with my friends. We had a party in a local hotel room where I passed out and the next thing I remember was waking up in the Flagstaff city jail.

Military life

I was officially inducted into the Army on May 4, 1966 in Phoenix, AZ. After passing the physical exams, I was sworn in, and a large group of us inductees were bussed to Sky Harbor Airport in Phoenix and flown to El Paso, Texas and nearby Fort Bliss army base. We arrived at our basic training facility barracks sometime after midnight. We were issued a uniform and some bedding, and told to go find a bunk bed and claim it before we had breakfast. At about 3:00 in the morning, we went to a chow hall where we were fed the famous army SOS breakfast, a.k.a. shit on shingles, a.k.a. chipped beef on toast. I must have been hungry since it actually tasted good to me. The first few days in the Army were spent getting yelled at, getting organized, getting yelled at, and getting our hair shorn to the scalp in less than 60 seconds. We took long series of aptitude tests and got immunized for a half dozen diseases that I had barely heard of. There had been some cases of contagious spinal meningitis in our camp so we were seated with one vacant chair between us to minimize any further occurrences of meningitis among the troops. I don't know if this was effective but if it wasn't, we would never hear about it.

Basic training seemed to be all about physical conditioning, marching in formation and hiking across hot, dry deserts. There was a lot of swearing and for some soldiers, physical hardships caused them more stress as they got yelled at and forced to do extra work. For some, the stress was too much and they either "flipped out" and became a basket case or they would just sit down or fall down and refuse to move anymore. I suppose if some men (boys) could not handle stress, it was better to find out in stateside training rather than in a Vietnamese jungle under combat conditions. I was young and skinny and in shape and I had no problems with the conditioning. My only concern was that I never got enough sleep.

I was assigned to the third platoon in a training company and precision marching was not our forte. Our drill instructors began calling us the "third herd" and this degenerated into us being called the "turd herd." Since many of the soldiers were draftees, we came from many varied backgrounds, racial groups, and educational levels so it was a never ending mix of human drama.

During our desert hikes we would march in the heat of the day in June and July in the hot Texas high desert country. We marched two abreast while a truck followed along behind the column. Every now and then, a soldier would collapse and fall face down in the desert sand. We stepped over them and continued marching as the truck picked up the fallen soldiers. At the end of some marches, there would be a truck load of exhausted soldiers following along behind the column. During our eight weeks of basic training, we were allowed one weekend pass and we all went into El Paso and marveled at the civilian world that we had been removed from six weeks earlier. Most of us were too young to drink and too poor to splurge but it was nice just to be off base in a civilian environment, not being yelled at and being able to eat some non army food. For the June, 1966, monthly pay period, as a private, E–1, I earned $87.90 minus collections of $15.99 which gave me a net monthly income of $72.30.

After basic training, we received our orders for our next assignment which was to receive advanced individual training (AIT), and we all went our separate ways on leave for a week or two. After our leave, we reported to our advanced training site and for me, this was radio operator school in Fort Ord, California, near Monterey and about 100 miles south of San Francisco. The training pace was still intense, but without the harassment we endured in basic training. We trained for a minimum of eight hours per day but had evenings and weekends off which was pure luxury after basic training.

We listened to Morse code four hours a day and once we could comprehend a slower speed, we would be raised to a higher speed and tested again for comprehension. Four hours a day was the maximum amount of "dits" and "dashes" we could endure because it soon became mind numbing. The remainder of each day was spent learning about radios and their operation, map reading, and related knowledge required to be a radio telephone operator. We also received two days of training on how to survive an ambush on a convoy in a simulated Vietnamese village. By this time, we all assumed that every one of us would be assigned duty stations in Vietnam. Some guys had the attitude that they could do anything they wanted to do and if caught, they would say 'What can the army do to me? Send me to Vietnam?"

On my twentieth birthday, my orders were posted on a bulletin board indicating that I was assigned to the First Air Cavalry Division based in Qui Non which was located north of Saigon, Republic of Vietnam. A few soldiers lucked out and received assignments to Germany or Korea or stateside locations but I estimated that over 80% of us received orders for Vietnam. I graduated from radio school and left Fort Ord on October 14, 1966, with a military occupational specialty (MOS) of O5B40, intermediate speed radio operator.

CHAPTER 2

SAIGON - CHAU DOC - AN PHU

After basic training in Ft. Bliss, Texas and advanced training in radio communications was completed in Fort Ord, California, I received my orders for Vietnam. After a short leave to say goodbye to family, friends and my girlfriend, I departed for Vietnam on October 31, 1966, leaving Travis Air Force Base in California and refueling in Anchorage, Alaska and Tokyo, Japan.

I clearly remember our descent into Saigon late at night on November 2, 1966. The city lights twinkled weakly in a sea of blackness that was the countryside and jungles surrounding Saigon. Upon deplaning the airliner and walking down the stairway ramp to the tarmac, I remember the sensation of heat and humidity on my skin and the smell of the city. It did not stink but it had a damp, earthy odor with a mixture of stagnant water, cooking food and busy city traffic. We lugged our duffel bags and personal gear onto a drab army green school bus with chicken wire covering all the open windows. A staff soldier on board the bus welcomed us to Vietnam and told us that the chicken wire was there to prevent hand grenades from being tossed into buses full of soldiers such as ourselves. After a 30 minute bus ride through the city, we arrived at Koelper compound which was formerly a civilian hotel that had been converted to military housing. I was pleasantly surprised to learn that I had become a private first class, PFC, E-3, upon entering Vietnam and that my orders had been changed. My initial set of orders before I left America was to be assigned to the First Air Cavalry Division headquartered in Qui Nhon which was north of Saigon. When I arrived in Vietnam, my new orders assigned me to a Military Assistance Command-Vietnam (MACV) advisory team in a place called An Phu District in Chau Doc Province located about 110 miles west of Saigon along the Cambodian border.

We were issued two pairs of olive green jungle uniforms along with two pairs of green and black jungle boots and our weapons. Since the Vietnamese troops were equipped with U.S. military surplus WWII weapons, we were issued similar weapons. I was issued an M-2 carbine which was a select fire, semi and full automatic, light weight, .30 caliber short rifle.

After a week of general orientation to Vietnam, I was deemed ready to proceed to An Phu. I was a twenty year old Native American who, until four years previously, had lived on Indian reservations my entire life so I was very apprehensive and uncertain about how and where I would end up. The learning curve under these circumstances was very high. I was totally focused on learning everything I could as fast as I could since my very survival was at stake. After returning to Tan Son Nhut airbase, I hitched a ride in a UHB-1 Huey helicopter to

Can Tho. From Can Tho, I hitched another ride to Chau Doc which was a Special Forces (SF) B team. The B team supported the Special Forces A teams and our camp in An Phu which was a converted SF A team staffed by regular Army soldiers.

The Special Forces B team housed about sixty soldiers. The non-commissioned officers in the "commo" department were radio communication professionals with many years of experience. They took me under their wings and gave me one week of training on all aspects of radio communications in our area of operation. I still remember a Sergeant Crow who was a great teacher and I am forever grateful for the training and mentorship he gave me to become a more capable radio operator.

In radio school in California, I had trained on WWII vintage radios but when I arrived in Vietnam, our troops were using completely different radios such as the PRC 25 (commonly called the " prick 25"). This was an excellent modern FM radio with digital tuning and depending on antenna configuration, it had a range of several miles to twenty miles in the flat delta region we operated in. It weighed 29.5 lbs and I became very familiar with this radio over the next eighteen months.

After a week of training at the B team in Chau Doc, I was ready to go to my assigned duty station. An Phu was located about six miles north on the Bassac river, which was a tributary of the nearby Mekong River. The U.S. Navy had river patrol boats (PBRs), which resembled the PT boats of WWII in shape and size. These boats were fiber glass and equipped with three .50 caliber machines guns and Starlight scopes which could see in near total darkness. The propulsion system was a jacuzzi water jet that enabled these boats to operate in very shallow water. These boats patrolled at night to interdict Vietcong movement of men and supplies.

A PBR boat crew picked me up in Chau Doc one night and after an uneventful six mile trip upstream, we made radio contact with An Phu team members on a small riverside dock. They began flashing a light and as our PBR approached the light, the boat crew armed their weapons just in case the Viet Cong (VC) had intercepted our radio calls. The atmosphere was tense until we closed to about 50 yards and greetings were exchanged in English.

Camp An Phu and Team members

I arrived in Camp An Phu in late November, 1966. Our official designation was the An Phu Sub- sector, Advisory Team # 64. An Phu district was very isolated and surrounded on the north, south and west by Cambodia. The Vietnamese designation for a local government unit was a district (i.e, county) and Chau Doc was a province (i.e, state). The military designation of a district was a sub-sector and a province was a sector. The camp was located on the far western side of Vietnam within 3,600 meters (2.1 miles) of the Cambodian border. The camp was a former Special Forces "A team" camp that had been staffed by Green Berets soldiers. In August, 1966, it was converted from a Special Forces A team to a MACV advisory team staffed by regular Army soldiers. The camp was staffed by about eight American advisors plus a contingent of Vietnamese officers and support staff numbering about ten members. The camp had two 155 mm howitzers with 20 additional Vietnamese artillery crew members. These were regular Vietnamese Army soldiers known as ARVNs (pronounced are- vins). The complete name was Army, Republic of Vietnam. The Vietnamese artillery commander had trained at Fort Sill, Oklahoma and spoke

English. Additional camp protection was provided by a Vietnamese Regional Force (RF) company that consisted of about 60 to 120 additional soldiers. The American advisory team consisted of a Commanding Officer (CO) usually a Major, an Executive Officer (XO), usually a Captain, and four to six senior, non commissioned officers who were Sergeants with ranks of E-6 and E-7. I was the youngest and lowest ranking member of the team initially being a private first class, E-3, and finally becoming a buck Sergeant, E-5, near the end of my tour of duty. For the most part, we were all treated as equals. Our officers did not require us to salute and we did not have to endure petty military bullshit that was prevalent in many stateside military installations. We all had our jobs to do and we did them.

My specific job was to maintain radio contact with our Special Forces B team (B-42) which was our support center located six miles south of us. I would send encrypted situation reports (sit reps) every morning summarizing any relevant activities and intelligence information that occurred over the prior 24 hours. We monitored our radio constantly, 24/7. I had to stay within earshot of the radio at all times or arrange for a team member to stay near our radio if I was not present. Regular voice communications could be handled by any team member but if messages needed to be encoded, I was the designated person to encode the messages and transmit them, primarily by voice, but sometimes by Morse code. I learned Morse code in training and I was proficient at medium speed but not at high speed. The senior communication sergeants were expert at high speed Morse code transmission but since our radio network was not very proficient overall, we would send messages at medium speed via Morse code, or more often, we would transmit our encrypted messages via voice. After 44 years, I still remember my military radio call sign which was "2XAW" or two, x-ray, alpha, whiskey. In Morse code it was *di di dah dah dah – dah di di dah -- di dah – di dah dah.*

For night coverage, all team members took turns on a rotational basis and stayed awake all night to monitor our radio. Our officers also took turns along with us enlisted men and the system worked well with each of us pulling night duty once a week. Besides monitoring the radio and making hourly contact with our B team, the night duty person would also check the interior perimeters of our living quarters to ensure our security. The outer perimeter had full time armed sentries so our interior patrol was less rigorous than that of the sentries. Another important function was to check on our kitchen to stop rats from stealing food which they did by chewing through the backs of wooden cabinets.

Our living quarters, sleeping quarters, office area and kitchen were arranged in two buildings that were approximately 30 feet by 60 feet in size. The exterior walls were made of galvanized metal sheeting surrounded by a four foot high gray concrete fence and the top half of each wall consisted of bamboo flaps which could be opened or closed as weather dictated. Green mosquito netting covered the upper interior walls all around the building. It had cement floors and the ceiling was constructed of PSP (perforated steel planking) covered with sand bags. Over the ceiling there was a galvanized sheet metal roof. This was supposed to withstand a direct hit from a mortar round and it seemed sturdy enough to actually do so. My room measured about 10 feet by 10 feet square and consisted of a single metal framed bed with mosquito netting, a small wooden desk and a bamboo closet. This was the first time in my life that I had my own private room and I was happy to have such accommodations.

The camp was constructed with a square perimeter that measured about l75 yards on each side. . There was an exterior six foot high earthen berm which was fortified with a shallow moat, concertina wire, punji stakes and claymore anti-personnel mines. South Vietnamese Regional Force (RF) soldiers provided security for the exterior perimeter. There was also an interior perimeter which was basically just a four foot high barbed wire fence which was not really any security at all. On the interior of this fence was where we American advisors lived along with our Vietnamese counterparts that consisted of a Major, a Captain, and some non-commissioned officers. Two l55mm howitzers were also located in the compound interior. In the center of our compound was an elevated command bunker which was our doomsday bunker where we would retreat to if we were overrun during an attack. There was an underground communications bunker where I would maintain radio contact and over head was an elevated area protected with sandbags. This square bunker measured about ten yards on each side.

During my eighteen month tour of duty, I served under three Commanding Officers (CO). Major Spade was my first CO and an excellent officer. He had seen duty in WWII and Korea and after a break in service, reactivated his commission for Vietnam. He was a fair man and provided good leadership. He wasn't into strict military discipline but insisted that we all do our jobs well. He was a good commander but within six months he was promoted to a lieutenant colonel and left our camp to assume another job in our higher headquarters located in Sadec, fifty miles distant. He was my favorite CO as he helped me get my accelerated promotion which I was always thankful for.

Our second CO was Major Engles. He had been reassigned from another command in Vietnam for reasons unknown to us. He was a very professional, hardcore soldier. Ranger trained and an expert in Tae Kwon Do karate, he was strict but fair and the speculation was that he had encountered problems at his former command with the Vietnamese political system. American officers had to be exceedingly good ambassadors and have good diplomatic skills to survive in Vietnam, particularly if you were assigned duty as an advisor to the Vietnamese army as we were. Major Engles was an excellent military officer but he may have been lacking in the requisite diplomatic skills and flexibility when working with the Vietnamese as an advisor. We did not know for sure why he was reassigned to our camp but he seemed embittered by his experiences in Vietnam

My next CO was Major Henry. He had served as an enlisted man in Korea and was awarded the Silver Star for combat bravery. He won a battlefield commission and he was a good, adventurous, extroverted officer who was more lax in discipline than our prior COs. He hated being stationed in Vietnam in an advisory role where there was little chance of any major combat action, which he desired. He had a brother in the Army who was stationed in Korea and he believed he could get approval to leave Vietnam since he thought two siblings could not be serving overseas at the same time. He submitted his transfer request and said his good byes to our team and left for Saigon and home (he thought). He returned a week later and very sheepishly told us that his transfer request had been denied since his brother in Korea was not in a combat zone. Apparently, a second sibling could be exempted from serving in a combat zone if another sibling was already in a combat zone. He lost a lot of respect from our team members since we all wanted to go home but we had twelve month commitments to fulfill.

Our team generally had about four to six senior non-commissioned officers who were sergeants, E-6 or E-7. Sergeant First Class (SFC) Wendell was a 20 year plus veteran who had been stationed in post WWII Italy and fought in the Korean war. In addition to his regular duties as a military tactics advisor, he was our unofficial senior counselor for all of the team members and could always be counted on to listen to issues and provide advice if requested. He became involved in identifying local children with cleft lips (i.e. hare lips) and referring them to an Australian surgical team that repaired their facial deformity. The lives of these children were dramatically changed for the better by these efforts. Sergeant Wendell told the story of how impoverished the Italians were after WW II and related how he had once gone into a nearby village and traded a Hershey chocolate candy bar for sex. When he returned to camp, he bragged to his buddies about his trade and they became upset with him because he had inflated the cost of sex since they had previously been trading half a chocolate bar for sex!

SFC Gunnison was a former Army Special Forces Green Berets who had returned to duty in the regular Army. Regular Army service was more compatible with maintaining a family life since deployments overseas were not as frequent as those of the Special Forces units. He was trained in weapons and explosive ordnance and he was our resident expert when it came to maintaining our defensive perimeter with claymore mines or blowing something up. When you went into the field in a dangerous area, it always felt good to have SFC Gunnison with you. He insisted on carrying an M-14 rifle with a bipod which was a good, heavy, long range rifle chambered for the .308 caliber round. He was a courteous, soft spoken man that had a quiet intensity about him that said he was super competent and capable. He was a model soldier embodying all that was good about professional US Army soldiers.

SFC Swain was our supply officer and manager of our camp support staff. He was a black man on his third tour in Vietnam and had a Vietnamese girlfriend in Can Tho which was about sixty miles distant down the Bassac River. He seemed to prefer the life style we lived in Vietnam rather than endure the racial discrimination that was still rampant in parts of America, particularly in the south. He was a quiet, introverted man, but a very pleasant companion once you got acquainted with him. He had contacts throughout Vietnam and it was amazing what he could procure through his informal supply channels. It was always a pleasure to accompany him on our food supply quests, particularly, when we went to Saigon for supplies.

We had two Navy two medics assigned to our team during my extended tour in Vietnam. They were called "*bac si*" (doctor) by the Vietnamese. Navy medics generally were assigned to ship or shore duty in big naval bases near urban areas so it came as a shock to them when they received assignments to small army advisory teams stuck in remote places like An Phu, a hundred miles from the sea. They had good attitudes about their assignments and were superbly trained. They had an ample supply of medicine and equipment to provide basic health care for our team members. They conducted community health clinics in our district and provided a crucial service that was very popular with civilians, particularly women and children.

I was stationed in An Phu for twelve months and then extended my tour another six months so I served almost eighteen months; November, 1966 through April of 1968 in Vietnam. Over these eighteen months, I saw our team members rotate at least once and sometimes twice. I was the longest serving team member when I left and I would have to say that over 95% of our team members were outstanding soldiers and good human beings who were there to do their job and go home and get on with their lives. Racism was not a major issue. Drugs were not an issue and none of our team members smoked marijuana. Alcohol usage was a weekend thing we did in camp. There were very few problems within our team other than one fight and a couple of arguments which were resolved by the next morning

Vietnamese Soldiers

Our Vietnamese counterpart, Major Phan, was an extremely competent career officer who was well respected by his soldiers and the local villagers. Major Phan was a Hoa Hao Buddhist and the vast majority of the Ah Phu population was Hoa Hao. This Buddhist sect was strongly anti communist and was a major factor that allowed our sub sector to be relatively safe and quiet. We were located in an area surrounded on three sides by Cambodia, which was supposed to be a neutral country but was, in fact, an enemy sanctuary. Major Phan spoke fluent English and French and was a very affable and effective officer who worked well with our team. There were several lower ranking Vietnamese Captains and junior officers that served with him but their English was very limited and we interacted less with them because of the language barrier.

The Vietnamese military had several different categories of Army soldiers in addition to having Air Force and Navy components. The regular Vietnamese Army troops were known as ARVNs The only ARVN soldiers we had in our area were the artillery crew based in our camp and they numbered about 20. The next category of soldiers was the RF (Regional Force) soldiers that were comparable to the US Army National Guard except these soldiers were on duty for the duration of the war. One and sometimes two companies of RF soldiers provided camp security and numbered from about 60 to 120 men. The next category of soldier was the PF (Popular Force) soldiers, who lived in their local village areas, often with their families. I compared them to the "Minute Men" soldiers or citizen soldiers who worked part time as farmers but also had military duties. The Special Forces A team before us had employed local soldiers known as CIDG (Civilian Irregular Defense Group). These soldiers were paid monthly and could quit the military whenever they wanted by turning in their weapon and uniforms. In our area, many of the CIDG soldiers converted to RF soldiers when Camp An Phu converted from SF to MACV in August, 1966. The ARVN were the best trained soldiers, while the RF were next in level of training and the PF were considered the least trained. The RF and PF troops were generally from the local area and seemed more motivated to fight for their community and family once a fight was unavoidable. The RF and PF soldiers were issued WWII American weapons. The smaller M-1 and M-2, .30 caliber, carbine was a good size for the small statured Vietnamese soldiers who would typically weigh about 110 to 150 pounds. Other soldiers carried the M-1 Garand which was a full sized, heavier rifle. The most macho of the Vietnamese soldiers wanted to carry the BAR (Browning automatic rifle) which was considered a light machine gun and weighed close to 20 pounds. The other choice weapon of the macho soldiers was the Thompson sub machine gun, .45 caliber, which weighed about 15 pounds and was most effective in close quarters combat.

Camp life

A routine day in camp consisted of getting up at 0600 (6 AM) hours, sometimes taking a cold shower, shaving and dressing for breakfast at 0700 hours. I shaved about once per week. I would send out my encoded report over our radio by 0800 hours. Depending on intelligence reports and the whims of our Vietnamese counterparts, our team members would go on combat patrols, community development inspections, conduct medical clinics for local villagers, inspect Vietnamese military outposts and provide advice or assistance as appropriate. We also did community relations work with local government officials. At least once or twice weekly, members of our team made a mail run and resupply trip via boat or jeep/ferry to our B team. We never traveled alone and sent a minimum of two team members out and sometimes three depending on the area traveled.

About once a month, we sent two team members to buy food for our team from an American post exchange store (PX). This was a favorite trip and our supply sergeant would take one team member with him to help haul the food back to camp. Sometimes we would go to Saigon and that was a vacation for us. We would spend several days there enjoying the sights and sounds of the city. The actual food purchasing only took a few hours but the difficult part was arranging transportation by truck to the airport and then a flight back to our camp or a nearby town. The Saigon bars and women were fantastic and the pace of life in Saigon was full speed, go-go around the clock. Many Americans stationed in and near Saigon performed mainly administrative support missions and they never had a chance to go into the field. Some of them wore tailored camouflage jungle fatigues and had a bayonet strapped to their boot or lower leg. We referred to these soldiers as "Saigon Warriors" and they were usually the drunkest and most boisterous guys in the local bars. There were military bars for Americans only and beer cost 10 cents per can and mixed drinks, 25 cents per drink. Cigarettes cost $1.00 a carton with a ration card. Prices were so cheap, we felt obligated to smoke and drink.

Our team was not supported by the regular Army supply system but we were given a cost of living allowance (COLA), of $79 monthly. We all contributed our allowance monthly to buy our food and provide a salary for our two "hooch" maids, Co Mau and Co Bah, and our general maintenance men who were a father and son team. We ate a combination of American food purchased at Army PXs and local fish, chicken and vegetables including a lot of rice. We pumped water out of the nearby river and treated the water with chlorine and alum to settle out the sediment (dirt). I do not believe we ever got sick from our camp water although all team members often had diarrhea during the entire time we were in Vietnam. The other possible cause of our diarrhea was the weekly anti malaria pill we took to prevent malaria. We routinely ate local food with no ill effects and only occasionally experienced acute diarrhea which was painful and debilitating for a day or two. For most team members, our bodies adapted to the local food.

The weather was either, warm, hot or wet. During the Summer, we had a monsoon season and every afternoon, like clockwork, we received a heavy down pour for at least a couple of hours. After the rainstorm, the clouds lifted and the setting sun painted the billowing clouds in the western skies with brilliant hues of gold, orange and pink. Cameras pictures never did the scenes justice as much as we tried to photograph the sunsets. After the summer monsoon season, we would have a mild but warm Fall and Winter season. The Spring would warm up and get hot and dry until the summer monsoon rains came and the cycle was repeated.

We did not have hot water unless we built a fire and heated up a barrel of water. If we wanted a shower, we waited until the warmest part of the day and then took one. Our camp was about five feet above the nearby river water table so drainage of sewer was always a problem. To facilitate drainage and minimize sewer waste, we used toilet paper but did not put it in our water operated flush toilets. We placed our soiled toilet paper in a can beside the toilet and each morning, our maintenance man would burn the used tissue. Over time, this became a habit and when we left our camp area, we had to remind ourselves to flush soiled toilet paper. One of our team sergeants went to Hawaii to meet his family during his R & R and stayed in a very nice hotel. When he returned, he told us that on more than one occasion, he had dropped soiled toilet paper on the floor beside the toilet which mortified his wife.

During March, 1968, I received a monthly salary of $373. This amount consisted of base pay for a buck sergeant, (E-5), which was $211 per month. We received additional pay for serving in Vietnam (which was not considered a desirable duty station) plus hostile fire pay (for getting shot at), and the

COLA so we could buy our own food. While this does not seem like a lot of money, it was for me at that time. Most of our team members received much higher pay since they had advanced rank plus many years of service and additional pay for critical military specialty occupations. We really had no place to spend our money. We would buy an occasional meal or beer from a local village but this cost amounted to no more than $20 or $30 per month. We received payment in MPC's, military payment certificates, (aka "funny money"). We were not supposed to possess or use American money since these dollars could be used on the black market and could aid enemy purchases of supplies for their efforts. The Vietnamese vendors took MPC's the same as US dollars so it did not matter to US troops how they were paid. The pay of American troops was much more than that of their Vietnamese counterparts. It was approximately 10 times greater than the equivalent pay that a Vietnamese soldier received of comparable rank. Most of our team members saved over half of their pay as an allotment which they received when they left Vietnam or the Army.

Over time, I developed mixed emotions about our communications bunker which I used to send and receive encrypted Morse code messages. One night, I went down into the "commo" bunker which measured about five feet by six feet to receive a message. As I reached into my desk drawer to get a message pad, a startled rat ran across my hand and arm. On another occasion, I went into the bunker in the middle of the night to receive another message. I was half awake staring at the floor waiting for the incoming message when I saw a snake head appear in the corner of the floor at the wall. We stared at each other for a few seconds before it retreated. It was four feet from me. If the snake had proceeded into the bunker, I was prepared to jump vertically about four feet as I made my escape. I was wide awake after that encounter, and every time after that, when I had to enter the "commo" bunker to take messages.

The first Vietnamese word I learned was "*cha'o,*" which meant" hello." The second and third words I learned were "*toi doi*" which meant "I am hungry". Over a year and a half, I learned enough Vietnamese to speak the rudimentary language and I assisted in teaching an English language class to Vietnamese soldiers and civilians for several months. As a joke, I would tell people in Vietnamese that I was Vietnamese but I was born in America and came to Vietnam in the US Army and was relearning the language. This was always good for a laugh and our interpreter made sure everyone knew we were joking. Over eighteen months, we had two Vietnamese interpreters assigned to us. They were invaluable members of our team and provided a crucial communication link to our Vietnamese counterparts and community members.

The Vietnamese troops also had the equivalent of a USO entertainment group. On rare occasions, they would come to our area to perform for the local Vietnamese troops. The Vietnamese USO group would usually consist of about six men and women performers. They arrived in a boat with costumes and portable sets and a small electric generator to power the microphone and speakers. A couple of our team members would go out to help with security while they performed. Between performances, we visited with the performers who were very adept in English. They invited us to a picnic of fresh snails and other delicacies. One Vietnamese lady in her mid twenties thanked us Americans for helping her country fight the communists. She gave me a small gold necklace with a

Christian cross as a token of her thankfulness and friendship which I had for many years. I can't recall her name but she is not forgotten. Our platonic friendship was an intense meeting of friends joined together in a common cause. I admired this troupe that was unarmed and risking their lives to entertain the Vietnamese troops. The Viet Cong routinely killed groups such as these that were helping boost the morale of the Vietnamese troops. They performed that night and departed the next morning. They were gentle and brave people.

Our primary mode of transportation was by boat. Our team had two 14 foot outboard motor boats that were stable and fast. We also moved about our area of operation and beyond by hitching rides on US Navy PBR patrol boats or Vietnamese Navy WWII landing craft boats which had the front ramp that could be lowered to off load vehicles. Our least favorite water transport mode was small sampans which were very unstable for heavy, uncoordinated American soldiers. We could only go short distances by road since our area was laced with rivers and canals, many of which did not have bridges or ferries. We had a jeep and a ¾ ton truck which we used sparingly. Our favorite mode of transport was by aircraft which almost always meant the UH -1, Huey helicopter that seemed to be flying everywhere, all the time. These helicopters cruised at almost 100 miles per hour, and would fly in a straight line point to point and land anywhere. Occasionally, we would catch a ride in an Army cargo/transport aircraft such as a Caribou or an Air America STOL aircraft. I remember one instance where there were a large number of us enlisted troops waiting to leave Can Tho for Saigon. There was a Caribou leaving but it had no seating equipment. The crew chief told us to sit on the aircraft floor, six abreast, with our legs extended. He then lashed us down with a four inch wide cargo strap to keep us secure for our short flight of thirty minutes. Air America was the private American airline company that served the CIA as its primary customer. They had white aircraft and their own radio frequencies. They flew into and out of Cambodia with no local radio contact with American military installations. We could only wonder where they were going or what they were doing.

Early in my tour, there was one particular incident that became a valuable learning experience for me. I and another American sergeant accompanied a Vietnamese patrol on an overnight inspection of one of the local Vietnamese border outposts. After the day's work was done, we ate with the Vietnamese soldiers and drank with them. The sergeant I was with liked to drink a lot and I joined in for the evening festivities. The next thing I remember was waking up the next morning in a foxhole where I had passed out the night before. I realized that I had been completely incapacitated because of alcohol and could not have functioned if we had been attacked. I could have woke up dead that morning. As it turned out, there were no serious consequences of our drunken behavior but I learned a valuable lesson from this episode and I had only myself to blame for not controlling my drinking. I knew that the consequences of my lack of control could have been deadly for me and my fellow American and Vietnamese soldiers. I could not blame my fellow sergeant for what happened even though he drank to excess also. I took this lesson to heart and during the rest of my tour, I never drank to excess again and was always competent to do my job by limiting my intake of alcohol.

Our closest, higher HQs was the Special Forces B team, (B–42), located six miles distant in Chau Doc. The main room on the ground floor in this HQs building contained a large bar that resembled the bar in the movie *Casablanca*, both in atmosphere and cast of characters. There were many Green Berets soldiers, with or without their beret, and us regular Army soldiers in green jungle fatigues that were considered second class soldiers. The elite Navy SEAL soldiers wore various camouflage uniforms and then there were an assortment of "civilians" lounging about in the bar. Some of these "civilians" were truly civilians working for USAID, CIA and other American civilian agencies. Other men were dressed in civilian clothes and were technically civilians, with previous military backgrounds, that worked for the "Project Phoenix" counter terrorism program. This project was classified at the time but is now a matter of public record. They basically did the same thing that the Viet Cong cadre did but in reverse. The Viet Cong would routinely assassinate local elected and appointed Vietnamese government officials and would then install their own communist officials and set up a communist shadow government. Project Phoenix staff would eliminate the communist shadow government leaders It was understood what these men did but it was never discussed nor were they ever asked direct questions about what they did.

There were about a half dozen American nurses working in a local hospital in Chau Doc and their arrival at the bar on rare occasions was a happening with every American soldier wanting to meet and woo them. We called them "round eyes" and it was so unusual to see a Caucasian woman that we would talk about them for days afterward as if we had seen a rare human species. There were also several beautiful Vietnamese bar hostesses that worked in this bar but they were strictly off limits which made them even more desirable.

A Navy SEAL (Sea, Air, Land) team was stationed in Chau Doc and occasionally they would operate in our area. They were elite warriors who operated very independently and practiced unconventional warfare with specialized weapons. The SEAL team operating in our area would patrol into Cambodia at night and do reconnaissance on enemy troop movements. They would locate and follow a VC patrol and transmit position coordinates to me and I relayed these coordinates to our Vietnamese artillery crew who fired 155 mm flare rounds to illuminate areas near the VC troop location for observation and harassment purposes. Cambodia was normally a safe haven for VC troops as they moved north and south along the Cambodian side of the Vietnam border. Some SEAL team members carried 10 gauge pump shotguns while others carried silenced .45 caliber sub machine guns which sounded like a small cap gun when fired. They also carried Stoner light machine guns which fired the smaller .223 caliber round. The smaller round allowed one man to carry this mini machine gun with more ammo than could be carried with the much heavier M–60 machine-gun. The M-60 fired the larger .308 caliber round and was considered a crew serviced weapon. The SEALS also utilized specially trained German Shepherd dogs which could see and hear better than any human. The SEALs were elite fighting troops and the most highly trained warriors that I saw in Vietnam. Their "esprit de corps" bordered beyond arrogance. They were good and they knew it. The Army Green Berets were elite troops also but due to the rapid expansion of the organization during the war, many of the younger soldiers did not have the experience or extensive training that the more senior Green Berets possessed.

The Lonely Sergeant

I first met Sergeant George Walker in the bar at the Special Forces, "B team" compound in Chau Doc, in mid 1967. I would visit the compound once a week when our team made our supply and mail run from Camp An Phu. The compound was dominated by a large, old two story French colonial building. The central portion of the ground floor featured a large bar with a high ceiling and fans pushing the warm sluggish air around the room. Chau Doc was located on the Bassac river near the Mekong River where it flowed out of Cambodia. This southwest corner of Vietnam was where we fought our part of the Vietnam War.

Upon seeing SFC George Walker in the bar for the first time, it was obvious to me that he was a Native American. He was sitting by himself at a small table in the bar and I went over to him and introduced myself. We were probably the only two Native Americans in that part of Vietnam or at least he was the only other Native American I had met in Vietnam at that time. Being Native American, I wanted to talk with him and seeing that I was Native American, he tolerated my company. Sergeant Walker was a quiet Native American man with a broad craggy face that could be called ruggedly handsome. He had a light complexion and wore a pair of the standard army issue grey plastic framed glasses. We exchanged the usual information about where we were from and our tribal backgrounds. He was a Choctaw from Oklahoma and I was a Navajo/Seminole from Arizona. Sergeant Walker was typical of many young Native American men. After finishing high school, he couldn't afford nor did he desire to attend college but he wanted to see the world and like many restless young men looking for excitement and adventure, he joined the Army in 1949. Sergeant Walker was a large man, standing six foot tall and weighing at least 200 pounds. Despite his baggy jungle fatigue uniform, it was obvious that he was powerfully built but he had a sensitive nature about him. As I became acquainted with him, I came to realize that he was a casualty of a previous war America had fought.

It might have been the second time I met him that we had a beer or two and he started talking. After 44 years, I cannot remember the exact words spoken by him but the following is the best recollection I have of our conversations.

"I don't really like to be around black people and I don't really trust people very much so I just drink alone and don't mix much," he confided in me.

He told me this in a way that I understood and presumed didn't include me, because of our common Native American heritage. He was relaxed and talkative whenever we met. There is a certain bond between Native Americans which grows stronger when we are removed from our native surroundings and are thrust into a totally non-Indian world. Sergeant Walker told me that he had been an infantry rifleman in Korea when the communist North Korean People's Army (NKPA) invaded South Korea in the summer of 1950. He related the following story to me.

"I was stationed in Korea in 1950 and we were on the front lines south of the 38th Parallel. In the summer of 1950, we were attacked by the North Koreans one night without any warning and it was an all out attack along our entire front line.

"After fighting all night, we were running low on ammunition and the North Korean troops just kept coming. My buddies and I could tell that some nearby positions were getting overrun and we were worried that the North Koreans would surround us and we would be trapped. We had heard stories about how the Koreans treated POWs and we wanted no part of that. After we saw our troops on both sides of us get overrun, we decided to retreat back to our own lines so we would not get captured. We left our positions and were on the run most of the morning. I had a good friend who was a black guy with me and at mid day, he twisted his ankle on a rock. He told me he couldn't run anymore and wanted me to help him. He was my buddy so I helped him by carrying him on my back the rest of that day."

"Everything was confused," he continued," We were unsure of exactly where our lines were and toward evening, North Korean troops saw us and began chasing and shouting at us. My legs were starting to cramp up and I finally put my friend down and told him that I was sorry but I couldn't carry him any farther. My buddy gave me this wild eyed look and without saying a word to me, he took off running faster than I could run! He didn't even look back to check on me. I tried to follow him but my legs were pooped out from carrying him and the North Koreans caught me a couple of hours later. I never saw him again. I don't know if he lived or died but he didn't get captured with my group. I just couldn't believe how he had lied to me and used me and screwed me in the end. That's why I don't like blacks or trust people anymore," he said.

The sergeant got silent for a moment as if he was composing himself, but I sensed that he had more to say so I remained silent, waiting for him to continue.

"After we got captured, we were marched north to an area where the North Koreans had a POW camp. The Koreans were very strict with us and some of our guards were totally sadistic. After interrogation, we were of no further use to them and we were put in an internment camp further north to serve out the war. They let us grow vegetables but we had to share our crops with the guards and sometimes we were put in cages that were so small that we couldn't stand up. Over time, I developed such a hatred for my buddy who I had totally trusted. I decided it was safer for me to trust no one and only depend on myself and that is how I started operating as a POW. After the truce was signed, we were released and returned to the US Army and after some medical treatment and a long leave, I came back to active duty."

"Ever since that time, I don't really like or trust people," he confided in me.

Being captured by the enemy is a fear all soldiers have but rarely verbalize. My young, immature thoughts were that I couldn't be captured because I was invincible with my rifle and grenades and support of the most powerful Army in the world, the U.S. Army. But here, in front of me, was a powerful Native American warrior who had been captured and had survived and come back to fight in another war. I was fascinated by his story and knew deep inside myself that capture was possible despite all of my resolve not to let it happen. Capture was probably preferable to death but you could never be sure if capture didn't mean torture and then death.

Sergeant Walker and I remained drinking acquaintances until we finished our tours of duty and left Vietnam in 1968. I never saw him again but I have sometimes wondered where he is and what he is doing. I'm sure that he retired from the Army sometime in the 1970's. He carried a huge burden of the loss of faith in his fellow man and I like to think that he went home to Oklahoma and found peace and a restored faith in humanity.

Many tribes have warrior purification rites after a warrior returns from war and Sergeant Walker probably had a ceremony done for himself by his family members. These ceremonies cleanse the spirit of returning warriors who have experienced death and powerful negative forces.

I am sure that Sergeant Walker had such a ceremony.

Camp An Phu humor

Depending on the situation, we were on duty 24/7 but on a day to day basis with no crises in our area, we maintained a six day work week with Sunday off for personal time. If there was major enemy contact, we were automatically on duty for the duration but this occurred infrequently. After doing our assigned duties, we had a lot of free time that we could use at our discretion.

A couple of team members had adopted pets. One sergeant had a pet grey spider monkey that stood about a foot tall. We kept the monkey chained to an eight foot tall pole which had a wooden ammo box mounted on top as his house. This monkey had a very pleasant disposition and would readily come to humans and would interact with cows and dogs in a very amicable manner. Our Executive Officer (XO) adopted a female dog that lived under his bunk bed and she eventually had puppies. Once these puppies were old enough, they would go outside and play for hours with our friendly spider monkey tethered to a ten foot long chain

One day, another team member decided to buy another spider monkey as a companion for the one we had. After a short search, he found and purchased a monkey of the same species and size, but we came to find out later, it had a totally different and terrible temperament. It immediately started fighting with our "good" monkey and it became known as our "bad" monkey. We set up another pole for the bad monkey and allowed the tether chains to overlap by only one foot. In this manner, the monkeys could interact if they desired but if the bad monkey became aggressive, the good monkey could move back one foot and be out of reach. The XO's puppies quickly became aware of the bad monkey's temperament as he would attempt to choke them whenever he got his hands on them. The puppies were very careful to avoid the bad monkey and play only with the good monkey.

One evening, someone, never identified, decided to switch the two monkeys from their adjacent poles. The next morning, the puppies came trotting out to play with the good monkey which was actually the bad monkey. The bad monkey immediately tried to choke the puppies which caused a great commotion. The mother dog and the XO came racing to rescue the puppies. There was a lot of barking and profanity as the crisis was resolved. No one ever confessed to this deed but we had our suspicions.

There was another team that wanted to have a camp mascot so they pooled their money and sent a team member to Saigon to find and purchase a mascot. There was one street in Saigon that specialized in selling all kinds of wild and domestic pets. The sergeant finally decided on a small, beautiful jungle cat that had black spots on his tan coat. The proud sergeant bought a nice cage and took the jungle cat back to his camp. After a few weeks, the jungle cat's spots began to fade. After a month or two, it became obvious that the sergeant had paid good money to purchase a Saigon domestic alley cat that had been daubed with black shoe dye.

Much of our camp life was routine and boring but every now and then, there would be unusual events that we would find humorous, even if after the fact. We all took turns pulling night duty and did this about one night per week. The primary duty was to maintain voice radio contact with our higher HQs and to generally watch over our sleeping rooms and our kitchen so rats would not get into our food supply which was kept in a wooden cabinet. One night, our CO was on night duty when he caught a rat between the wall and the back of our food cabinet where it was chewing a hole into the cabinet. The rat was cornered and the CO did not want it to escape so he pulled his .25 caliber derringer and shot it at point blank range. Not one team member woke up. On another occasion, our interpreter was on night duty and he caught a rat in our food cabinet. He grabbed an arrow and stuck the rat by hand, without a bow. These were healthy country rats that could be 12 inches long, including their tails.

In our sleeping barracks, we had a resident lizard that was at least a foot long and it made a scratchy noise as it crawled around at night. We could never catch it and only glimpsed it 3 or 4 times and we suspected that it lived in our laundry room. The rationale was that it ate all the local insects in our barracks so it was a beneficial guest and we tolerated him/her.

We were confined to our camp at night, but during holidays such as Thanksgiving or Christmas or New Year, we would have a dinner party and host our Vietnamese counterparts. The Vietnamese were fond of proposing toasts, particularly for new American team members. A Vietnamese soldier would propose a toast and he and the American would each down a shot of cognac or scotch. Then another Vietnamese soldier would propose another toast to the same American and after a few rounds, the American would be drunk while a half dozen Vietnamese soldiers had only one drink each. Our interpreter was very skillful at bridging our communication gap and a fun time was generally had by all.

There were almost never any women at these events. We had a policy of non-fraternizing with local village women because we lived next to a small village of less than 4000 people. For fun we would go outside and shoot off small flares and then put our rifles on full automatic fire and attempt to shoot down the flares. We never shot a flare down and fortunately we never accidentally shot anyone on the ground either.

On weekends, we would sometimes play all night poker games. If a lot of money was involved, some team members would be upset over their losses. To tone down our poker games, our CO imposed rules on the games which called for a maximum raise of one quarter per round and three raises per hand. This limited losses or winnings and it was not uncommon to wind up winning or losing one or two dollars after playing poker all night. This was not as exciting as the no dollar limit games but it helped preserve peace and harmony among the team members.

We lived alongside the Bassac River which was a tributary that flowed parallel to the nearby Mekong River. Most of our movement was by boat with a small amount of travel by jeep or truck on dirt roads that followed alongside the river. We had two Boston Whaler fiberglass 14 foot boats with outboard motors which we used for local transport. Several of us younger enlisted men decided that we wanted to learn to water ski so I volunteered to make some water skis. I acquired a sheet of plywood which I cut into strips and by boiling the tips of the plywood and using weights, I put a curved tip on the skis. A team member volunteered his civilian shoes which I attached to our skis and they were ready for use. To ensure we had adequate power, we mounted our two outboard motors on one of our motor boats.

One nice sunny afternoon, some of us younger team members took our water skis out and skied on the Bassac River which was at least 1/2 mile in width. Most of our team sort of learned how to water ski or at least got up to the surface of the water. There was much laughter and joking, but after this one glorious outing, our CO told us we could not water ski anymore. We never heard an explanation why, but I can now imagine his concern that one of us might drown or get shot while water skiing. It would not look good on his service record to have to file a report on how one of his team members was allowed to water ski in a hostile environment and accidentally or purposely died in the line of recreation. It was fun while it lasted.

Our camp was divided into three sections for security purposes. Our inner section was the most secure and occupied by our eight man American advisory team and about 30 Vietnamese soldiers. Surrounding us was an intermediate camp area that was the living quarters for the Vietnamese Regional Force soldiers and their families that sometimes lived with them. Outside of this section was the outer perimeter which was heavily fortified with barbed wire fences and concertina wire.

Our recreational opportunities were limited and a popular source of entertainment was movies when we could obtain them. These were the dark ages when movies arrived in metal canisters and consisted of several 12 inch reels of film. We had a small electric generator and a film projector for these occasions. The Vietnamese were great fans of the movies like ourselves and in order to share our movies with them, we built a rectangular wooden frame measuring about six foot square just above the fence line and attached a white bed sheet to it. In this manner, we could watch movies from our side of the fence and the Vietnamese troops and their families could watch the reverse image of the movie from the opposite side of the screen where they had built some wooden bleacher seating for these occasions. The picture quality was good and the only down side was that any letters would appear backwards but since the Vietnamese audience did not read or write English, this was not a problem for them.

There was one memorable night when we watched the movie *Lawrence of Arabia*. The movie started at dusk and it was supposed to be about three hours long and came with extra canisters of film. The first couple of reels were fine but the next reel had been rewound backward. We had no option but to rewind the reel by hand, using a pencil and finger power. More than one reel was rewound incorrectly but we were determined to see the entire movie so we rewound the reels as necessary and finished viewing the movie around 0500 hours in the morning, just as the eastern sky was turning pink.

The favorite movies of the Vietnamese were western movies involving cowboys and cavalry and American Indians. They imagined the movies as depicting the US Army as the cavalry and the Indians as the Viet Cong. Since the Indians generally got beat by the cavalry, they liked the idea that the Viet Cong was also being beat by the US Army and Vietnamese military. Using our interpreter, I explained to several different groups that I was an American Indian, the same as in the movies and it was true that Indians used to fight the US Army but we had quit fighting about 80 years earlier. Now, some Indians had joined the US Army to help the Vietnamese fight their enemies which used tactics similar to American Indians in the 1800s.

The big name entertainers like Bob Hope, Ann Margaret and the Playboy Playmate bunnies would tour the big US bases in northern South Vietnam and entertain thousands of soldiers, sailors, and airmen in one show. We never had a chance to see them but we did get to visit with Martha Raye and Robert Mitchum. Martha Raye had adopted our camp and the Green Berets years earlier and she was an honorary Green Berets with her own green beret and uniform with name tag. She was a warm, caring and salty tongued lady that could embarrass the most seasoned Army sergeant in our camp. She is gone now but bless her compassionate soul for the humor and good will she provided us.

The other celebrity we met was Robert Mitchum, who was a big name movie star in the 1960s. He had starred in a recent movie called *Thunder Road* which was about the southern moonshine business and he was one of the drivers in the movie delivering illegal moonshine. He arrived in a helicopter and spent a couple of hours with us, drinking beer and just bullshitting and telling us about Hollywood and the making of the movie. He was a warm, down to earth human being and we appreciated our chance to meet and visit with him. Bless his soul.

CHAPTER 3

COMBAT

The combat missions we conducted with the Vietnamese were usually confined to certain areas of our district that had known Viet Cong soldiers or sympathizers. We usually departed our camp at 0200 or 0300 hours in the morning to be in position for an ambush or sweep of an area before daylight. We prepared our gear the day before and I remember thinking that these missions were like the ultimate hunting trip where the game you were pursuing also had rifles and would shoot back. Big game hunting was never as dangerous as going out on patrol. When explaining this, years later to my civilian friends, the only comparable civilian hunting experience that might induce similar fear or excitement would be to hunt grizzly bears or Cape buffalo with a bow and arrow without any rifle back up.

As a radio operator, I was responsible for carrying our team radio (PRC 25) and sticking close to my commanding officer so he had radio communications with our higher headquarters and coordination with air support should it become necessary. This could become critical if we needed air or artillery support. I ensured that I had a fresh battery in my radio as well as a spare battery if needed. I cleaned my M-2, 30 caliber, carbine often to prevent jamming. The carbine is a lightweight, short rifle with a limited effective range but since I was already carrying a 30 pound radio on my back, I did not want any additional weight. I carried 200 rounds of ammunition in 15 and 30 round magazines which we called banana clips because of its curved shape. I also carried two M 26 fragmentation grenades, two smoke grenades and if available, an illumination grenade. We carried water with us and since we normally did one day missions, we only carried snack food. We did not carry tenting or bedding so we could travel lightly. Our missions would normally terminate by late morning or noon and if we were hungry we would find a riverside village food stand and buy a meal.

Khan Binh region

During my third month in Vietnam in January, 1967, our team accompanied a Vietnamese RF company on a search and destroy operation in the Khan Binh region. This area was adjacent to Cambodia in the northwest section of our district. In this area, the border with Cambodia was separated by a narrow canal. Intelligence sources reported that VC forces had established fortified bunkers on the Vietnamese side of the border and the Vietnamese RF mission was to remove any enemy combatants and destroy the newly constructed bunkers.

A reinforced Vietnamese RF company of about 100 men departed before daybreak to assume positions in preparation for an assault upon the enemy held positions. I accompanied our team's Executive Officer to the region at about 0900 hours. The plan was to link up with our Commanding Officer and the remainder of our team that was with the Vietnamese commander, Major Phan and his staff. The Vietnamese forces established themselves along a tree line east of the enemy positions preparing for a frontal assault across a dry rice paddy about 200 meters in width. The Viet Cong were entrenched west of this open field in newly constructed bunkers. The estimated enemy strength was thought to be about 20 to 30 men. The Vietnamese commander was in no hurry to order an assault and discussed getting American air support to soften up the target before the assault. This was a possibility but we were not a priority since the American units further north had the highest priority for air support before Vietnamese forces.

As the radio operator, I accompanied our Executive Officer toward the skirmish line. The forest was calm and brightly lit in many pale shades of green as the forest canopy filtered the strong sunlight overhead. Suddenly, there was the unmistakable "zip" of a bullet cracking nearby over our heads. A few green leaf fragments fluttered down around our heads. The bullet had missed us by two or three feet overhead but it was clearly meant for us. In training we learned that priority targets for enemy snipers were officers, radio operators and automatic weapons crews. I doubt that the VC sniper could see us that clearly in the forest but we were the only two tall Americans foolish enough to be walking upright within his field of fire. We immediately went into a running crouch for about 200 meters and joined up with our commanding officer and his Vietnamese counterpart. It was decided that we would wait for close air support and we would start our advance simultaneously with an air assault on the enemy tree line. After about an hour, air support arrived and helicopter gunships began their strafing runs. The Vietnamese company, accompanied by us five American advisors began our frontal assault across the dry rice paddy field toward the tree line to the west. The Huey gunships armed with 7.62 mm mini guns and 40mm grenade launchers made several strafing runs along the tree line west of our position. Charging across the open field, we were all firing into the tree line making it difficult to hear return fire which seemed to be light. Advancing about halfway across the open field, I tripped over a small hump in the ground and fell down. I can still remember the sweet, cool smell of the grass and the dirt as my face pressed into the earth. I had become separated from my Executive Officer.

After reloading, I rose and continued my advance toward the tree line, 100 meters distant. I remember seeing flashes from the tree line and firing at them. Later, I realized that some of my ammo magazines had tracer rounds in them and some of the flashes I saw were probably my own outgoing tracer rounds. The excitement in the heat of battle was confusing but I knew that the safest place to be was in the tree line and not out in the exposed open field so I advanced as fast as possible.

The assault felt like it lasted an entire morning but in reality it probably lasted no more than 15 minutes. As we approached the tree line, the Huey gunships were called off and we proceeded to secure our tree line positions. There were several freshly dug bunkers that measured four foot deep and six foot wide by twelve feet long. They all showed signs of recent abandonment just minutes before and were only half finished in construction.

The tree line was a narrow 50 meters wide and bordered the canal on the west side that was the boundary between Vietnam and Cambodia. All of the VC had abandoned their positions and used canoes to paddle across the canal to Cambodia and safety. Cambodia was technically neutral, but in reality, was a safe haven for the Viet Cong. We were not supposed to cross into Cambodia, at least not in a blatant manner in broad daylight (we did night patrols into Cambodia occasionally).

I reunited with my Executive Office and he radioed in his situation report to our headquarters. He reminded me that I needed to stay by his side at all times but he understood the excitement of our first major engagement. He had seen me fall and was relieved to know that I had not been hit.

We spent a couple of days in the Khan Binh region while the Vietnamese soldiers destroyed the Viet Cong bunker fortifications One Vietnamese RF soldier was killed (KIA) and several wounded (WIA). No Americans were wounded and no Viet Cong bodies were recovered which was usually the case since the Viet Cong would remove their casualties if given a chance, just as the Americans would.

As my first combat experience, it made an impression on me that I will never forget. I was surprised at how easy it had been for me to fire into enemy positions with no qualms or misgivings. It would have been more dramatic if I had seen enemy combatants close up as we were firing at them but this was not the situation. I had wondered what my reaction would be when I first came under enemy fire. I was personally pleased that I had not frozen but I was also a little dismayed at myself that I could shoot and attempt to kill another human being in such a casual manner. I remembered a high school English class discussion from about three years earlier, where we students were discussing the issue of murder. The prevailing thought among most students was that a person who took a life was probably mentally unbalanced. Someone in class brought up the issue of soldiers taking lives during wartime and it was finally agreed that people could take another human's life and not be mentally unbalanced.

During my tour in Vietnam, none of our immediate team members were wounded or killed but our B team suffered several casualties. The B team was attacked by a Viet Cong recoilless rocket launcher team which was located across a river near the Cambodian border. After firing several rounds at the B team HQs, the enemy withdrew into the safety of Cambodia. A radio telecommunications soldier was killed in this attack and his assistant was wounded. There was also an older "civilian" stationed at the B team that was a friend of some of our team members and he would come visit us on his days off. He was killed about three months after I left Vietnam in a firefight that our team was involved in near Chau Doc. Major Henry wrote to me to tell me of the event.

During one patrol, we encountered a Vietnamese unit that had wounded and captured a Viet Cong radio operator. He had an abdominal wound and some of his intestines were exposed but he was conscious and alert and was awaiting an American medevac helicopter. It was unusual to request a medevac for a wounded enemy soldier and the concern for this particular soldier stemmed from the fact that, as a radio operator, he would have valuable information about the Viet Cong radio and communication systems and it was expected that he would provide this information after recovery and interrogation. He looked to be about my age. We heard later that he died en route to a hospital.

Typical village children loved to pose for pictures.
An Phu District. 1967.

"Co Mau", one of two maids at Camp An Phu.

Teenage daughter of local An Phu Village photographer.

Regional Force (RF) and Popular Force (PF) soldiers with boat
crew along Bassac River – An Phu District – February, 1967.

Vietnamese soldiers and American advisers waiting for
pickup after combat patrol – An Phu District – 1967.

Viet Cong casualty (KIA) at the Phu Hoi Camp attack on April 5, 1967. This man was most likely a victim of the AC−47 gunship, known as "Spooky" or "Puff the Magic Dragon".

Typical villages and dwellings as seen
from the Bassac River – 1967.

Typical Chau Doc street scenes. 1967.

R Wood and Co Xu, school teacher, in An Phu District. 1967.

Celebrities in remote Camp An Phu! Robert Michum and
Martha Raye visited our team and we greatly appreciated
meeting and visiting with them. 1967.

Off to the Races! Camp mascots, "TJ" the good monkey and "Doofis" the trusty dog. 1967.

Author Ron C. Wood in Vietnam in mid- 1967.

R. Wood in Khan Binh region, January, 1967.
Foxhole was dug by exploding 155 mm artillery round.

Last week in Vietnam for R. Wood. April, 1968. Khan Binh
region. I was supposed to be too short to be getting shot at.

R. Wood home in Flagstaff, AZ on 05 MAY 66. Relief!

DETACHMENT B-42
5TH SPECIAL FORCES GROUP (AIRBORNE), 1ST SPECIAL FORCES
APO San Francisco, 96215

3 July 1967

SUBJECT: Letter of Appreciation

THRU: Sector Advisor
An Phu Advisory Detachment
APO US Forces 96215

TO: SP-4 Ronald C. Wood

It gives me great pleasure to commend you for your outstanding performance of duty while attached to this unit as a radio operator during the month of June 1967.

In all respects, you proved yourself to be a very capable operator. Many times, you proved you professional ability while handling medical evacuation, air strikes, as well as routine service messages processed by both voice and C.W.

Your relationship with the other radio operators and the members of the team was exemplary, as shown by the smooth operation of the radio section and the many friendships you developed while you were here.

I personally wish to thank you for a job well done and look forward to having you serve with Detachment B-42 again in the future.

ROBERT L. STILES
Major, Infantry
Commanding

Appreciation letter from our SF B team commander. 1967.

UNITED STATES MILITARY ASSISTANCE COMMAND

BY DIRECTION OF THE SECRETARY OF THE ARMY
THE ARMY COMMENDATION MEDAL

IS PRESENTED TO

SPECIALIST FOUR RONALD C. WOOD

For the performance of exceptionally meritorious service in support of the United States objectives in the counterinsurgency effort in the Republic of Vietnam during the period

October 1966 to September 1967

Through his outstanding professional competence and devotion to duty he consistently obtained superior results. Working long and arduous hours, he set an example that inspired his associates to strive for maximum achievement. The loyalty, initiative and will to succeed that he demonstrated at all times materially contributed to the successful accomplishment of the mission of this command. His performance of duty was in the best traditions of the United States Army and reflects great credit upon himself and the military service.

Army Commendation Medal presented to R. Wood. September, 1967.

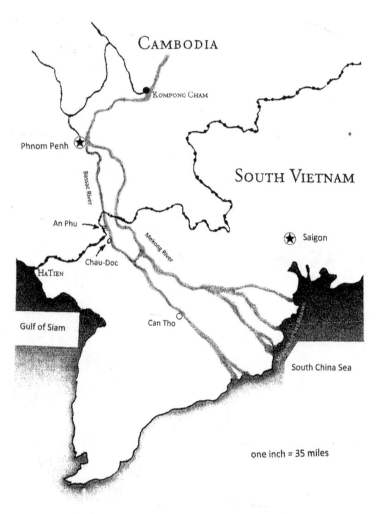

CAMBODIA

KOMPONG CHAM

Phnom Penh ⊛

Bassac River

SOUTH VIETNAM

An Phu →

Chau-Doc

Mekong River

⊛ Saigon

HA TIEN

Gulf of Siam

Can Tho ○

South China Sea

one inch = 35 miles

Detailed map of Southern tip of South Vietnam –
An Phu and Chau Doc

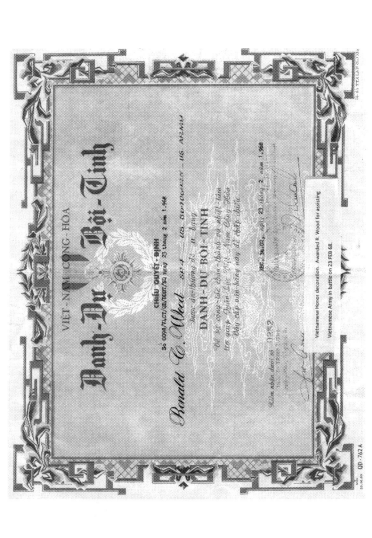

VIỆT - NAM CỘNG HÒA

Danh-Dự Bội-Tinh

CHIẾU QUYẾT - ĐỊNH
Số 0098/TLCT/SĐ/NĐ/PC số 23 tháng 2 năm 1.968

Ronald C. West   US. 56100425   US. ARMY

thuộc distribution 3/4 as in hang

DANH-DỰ BỘI-TINH

Vì sự công tác chặn - hành và nhiệt - tâm
trợ giúp Quân Lực Việt - Nam Cộng Hòa
Nay cấp cho hưởng này để chứt thưởng

Kèm nhật lãnh số 1252

Đạt 3h.00, ngày 23 tháng 2 năm 1.968

Vietnamese Honor decoration. Awarded R. Wood for assisting
Vietnamese Army in battle on 23 FEB 68.

NUMBER	PREFERENCE	CODED	DTG	FROM:	TO:
11	-O-	Y	051400	24	B42

SECURITY CLASSIFICATION

SITREP 94   GRC 206

041700 TO 051700 APR

PAR ONE A. 050125 APR. VC ATTK 450 RF CO LOC
PHU HOI VILL. VIC WS 066995. VC ATCKD FR
3 DIRECTIONS N, W, AND SW, EST 1 CO.
267 BN, STR 300. VC WPNS CONSIST OF
MORTARS, 57 RR, MG, B40 RCKTS AND ASA.
ASSORTED UNIFS. FRDLY CAS EST 67 WIA
15 RF KIA AND 23 CIV KIA. VC CAS,
31 KIA. US CONFIRMED. WIA UNK. VC WPNS
CAPTD 2 B-40 GREN LCHER, 3 US CARBINES.
1 M1 RIFLE. 050700 VC WITHDREW W.
B. 050130 APR. PHOUC HUNG VIC WS 195952
RECVD APPROX 22 RDS FR 82 MM MORTARS.
PSN OF MORTARS UNK. FRDLY CAS. 21 WIA.
C. ALL ACTION TERMINATED 050723.

PAR TWO. NEG

Copy of Situation Report transmitted on 05 APR 68. Phu Hoi battle.
An Phu District. After action report of battle to higher HQs.

SECURITY CLASSIFICATION

DATE		TOR		FILE		ACTION
APR		TOS 051550		R Wood		

137			072000	154
73				
B 42				

SpotRep 16

CLASSIFICATION

1. 072000 MAR 67 Dist Chief Rec Agent Rpt That Khanh An FOB, Phu Hiep FOB. (AND TAN CHAU OP) WILL BE ATTACKED. ARTY (AN PHU) PSN, Dist Town will be mortored. Also Tan Chau OP ONE (WILL BE ATK). MACV EVAL - C-3.

2. Ref VC mortar Attack 060220 Invest Revealed mortar Attack Consisted of 14 Rds 82mm Conif, 33 Cas Conif. 2 KIA, 31 WIA, only 1 Mil WIA, Ground Invest Reveal, VC Emplaced 2 mortars 82 mm (VIC) WT 082964 With Defensive positions. FR 084957 To 077968. VC Arrived At mort PSN 860130 And Fired 1st RD At 0220. Abandoned PSN 0330. Mort Type Conif by mort parts Found VIC WS 105957. Mort Fragments and other parts Forwarded To Your 02.

MAR	67	072232	
OFFICER Sent			
OPERATOR R. Wood			

Copy of Spot Report transmitted on 07 MAR 67. Local intelligence reported to higher HQs.

Honorable Discharge

from the Armed Forces of the United States of America

This is to certify that

WOOD RONALD C   527-64-1517   SGT   USAR

was Honorably Discharged from the

United States Army

on the   3RD   day of   MAY 1972   This certificate is awarded
as a testimonial of Honest and Faithful Service

LOUIS J. PROST
BRIGADIER GENERAL, USA

R. Wood Honorable Discharge document dated 03 May 72

(2 years active and 4 years in reserve)

Old Man Running

Khan Binh was a designated free fire zone in the northern section of our district and all the civilians had been relocated out of the area due to enemy presence in the area. Several months after the major operation just described, we returned to Khan Binh and entered into the free fire zone around 0300 hours in the morning with a platoon of Vietnamese troops and four American advisors from our team. The area was supposed to be devoid of any population. Any inhabitants were illegal, and presumed to be enemy Viet Cong and therefore free to be fired upon as enemy combatants. As a policy in a grim war, it sounds reasonable to deny the enemy the support and protection of the local populace. On this particular patrol, we entered the free fire zone just as the veil of night was lifting to give us a dim grey view of the countryside and a large pond about half the size of a football field next to a seemingly abandoned village.

Our section of the patrol consisted of about a dozen Vietnamese troops and two Americans. We all saw a man by the pond at the same instant. He was an old man, presumably a farmer, small in stature with long white whiskers and bare feet. He had on the common black pajamas that almost every country farmer wore and was squatting by the pond edge, washing his hands and face. The Vietnamese troops shouted at him to freeze and come closer. Instead this old man jumped up and started running along the pond bank angling away from us on the far side of the pond. The Vietnamese troops immediately opened fire on this old man with automatic and semi automatic rifles. The man was very quick and appeared to be running on top of the water along the pond edge. This happened in a matter of seconds but it was obvious to me that this old man was not a threat to us and he was unarmed. He was scared and trying to escape to survive another day. Bullets splashed all around him in the water and on the shore with none hitting their mark. I did not consider this old man a threat and I did not raise my rifle or even consider firing at him. This entire event lasted perhaps ten seconds but it plays out in slow motion in my memory. After sprinting about 30 meters, the old man reached a tree line and disappeared into the dim grey morning mist.

Ghoulish Gold

It was an accepted practice of some rural Vietnamese civilians and soldiers to have gold bridgework fitted to their teeth and dentures. It was explained to me that this was done as a sort of burial insurance policy because war time life was so unpredictable and your home and life could be destroyed in an instant by random events. The existence of a mouth full of gold fixtures could finance a decent funeral and burial.

A nearby Vietnamese outpost was overrun in April, 1967, and after the battle, which is described later, an American team went to the outpost to survey the damage and confirm the body count of 31 dead enemy combatants. Upon returning to our camp, one of our team members brought back a small bag of gold dental bridgework and fixtures which he had removed from the mouths of enemy bodies. He gave me a handful of these gold dental fixtures which I put into a sock filling it half full. I kept this sock for one day and I asked myself "Why am I keeping a sock of gold dental bridgework and fixtures taken from dead people?" I could not keep it. The next day, I gave the gold dental fixtures to our two "hooch" maids who were both war widows still raising children. This gold gift was welcomed by these ladies who had no qualms about profiting from the death of enemy soldiers who may have helped kill their husbands. I felt this was a 'win-win" situation whereby I helped two war widows out with badly needed financial assistance and I felt relieved and cleansed of having possessed dead people's gold belongings.

Sinking Sampan

During one morning patrol, we left camp in the early grey dawn and boarded a dozen small wooden sampans to cross the Bassac River to set up an ambush site. Sampans were small, round bottomed, ten foot canoes designed to carry two or three small statured Vietnamese. We used these sampans to avoid detection and maintain stealth as we moved into our ambush position. On this particular occasion, two Vietnamese soldiers and I were in one sampan complete with all of our combat gear. The Vietnamese soldiers carried M-1 Garand rifles with their combat gear and I carried a PRC–25 radio, along with an M – 79 grenade launcher and a load of grenades. I probably weighed a total of 230 pounds with all my gear on. We knew the sampan was fully loaded and we paddled carefully across the smooth, early morning river which was about one half mile wide. I was worried that the sides of our sampan were only about three inches above the water but we made it across the river without incident.

We set up our ambush but there was no contact and our mission was completed by noon so we began our return trip across the river. I noticed that the water had become rough and choppy due to the wind and river boat traffic. I had severe misgivings about this return trip so I removed my boots and called our team at the An Phu camp to let them know we were returning and to send out our motor boat just in case it was needed.

We made it about half way across the river when water started lapping over the sides of our sampan. I furiously bailed water out of the sampan with my helmet as I saw our team motorboat leaving the boat dock to come meet us. It was a losing situation and our sampan took on water faster than I could bail it out and our sampan began sinking. I slung my grenade launcher on my shoulder and grabbed my radio and boots in one hand and began to swim with my free hand but I could not stay afloat. I sunk underwater. I tried as hard as I could to surface with my equipment but I could not do it. I reluctantly released my radio and boots and was then able to surface and wave our outboard boat over to rescue me and the two Vietnamese soldiers I was with. I lost my boots, helmet and radio but I kept my grenade launcher with me. The Vietnamese soldiers lost their heavy M-1 Garand rifles. Later my team mates on the outboard motorboat that rescued me told me that they could see the sampan sinking and I was bailing water like crazy. Then the boat disappeared under the water and I was sitting in the middle of the two soldiers, still bailing water.

After returning to camp and drying out, I could see the humor of the situation but at the time I just felt fortunate not to have drowned. We returned to the river later in the day and attempted to dive for the lost equipment but the water was too swift and too muddy brown to see or find anything. Our equipment was considered combat losses and eventually replaced.

Phu Hoi Camp Battle

On April 5, 1967, at 0125 hours (1:25AM) the Viet Cong attacked a nearby camp located in the village of Phu Hoi about three miles northwest of our camp at An Phu. The Viet Cong attacked this village outpost from three directions, north, west and southwest. The Viet Cong strength was estimated at 300 men of the 267th Viet Cong battalion. The weapons they used were 82mm Chinese mortars, 57 mm recoilless rifles, machine guns, B–40 rocket grenades, locally manufactured claymore mines, and assorted small arms. Assorted uniforms were worn by the Viet Cong troops. Friendly casualties were estimated at 67 wounded, 15 Regional Force soldiers killed and 23 civilians killed (these were family members of the soldiers). Viet Cong casualties were 31 killed, (US Army confirmed) and an unknown number wounded. Viet Cong weapons captured were two B-40 grenade launchers, 2 US M-1 carbines, and 1 US M-1 Garand rifle. The attack lasted all night and terminated at 0723 hours in the morning when the Viet Cong withdrew west into Cambodia. Simultaneously, a nearby village of Phouc Hung was mortared with approximately 22 rounds of 82 mm mortar fire. Friendly casualties were 21 wounded. All action terminated at daylight the same day. This information came from one page of a situation report (sit rep) that I submitted to our HQs, B-42, on April 5, 1967.

As the report stated, the attack started at 0125 hours. We heard explosions from the battle and the Phu Hoi camp commander was constantly reporting by radio to our Vietnamese An Phu camp commander in our compound as the battle raged. We clearly heard battle noises in the background on the commander's radio as the situation became more desperate. The Vietnamese commander requested American gunship support to assist in the defense of the camp. The gunship was a vintage C-47 (DC 3) which mounted three 7.62 mm, six barreled electric gatling guns that could fire 3 to 6,000 rounds per minute. It was claimed that this gunship could put a bullet into every square foot of a football field within three seconds.

Toward morning (about 4 AM), the Phu Hoi camp commander arrived at our camp and reported that he had escaped from his camp on foot to report that his camp had been completely overrun by the Viet Cong. The An Phu camp commander requested that the approaching C-47 gunship fire directly into the camp since it was already overrun and occupied by the Viet Cong forces.

From our camp in Ah Phu, we saw the gunship in action. As the gunship fired, we saw red tracer rounds floating down to earth like delicate streams of red rain in the dark of night. There was an odd beauty to this scene, but knowing that 7.62 mm tracer rounds were creating this red rain, blunted any further thought of beauty. We knew that any life in the camp, friend or foe, would be killed by the deadly rain of bullets from the gatling guns. The enemy withdrew into Cambodia as dawn approached and Vietnamese and American team members entered the camp after daylight to confirm the damage and body count. I did not leave our camp since I was still completing my after action situation report that needed to be encrypted and sent to our higher HQs. Team members confirmed that many VC soldiers had been stitched by 4 or 5 bullets in a straight row from the gatling guns. The gun ship was nicknamed either "Puff the Magic Dragon" or "Spooky."

The day after the attack was over, a couple of Vietnamese trucks arrived at our camp and unloaded Vietnamese bodies from the Phu Hoi camp. The pile of dead bodies and body parts was approximately four feet high and ten feet in diameter. Why these bodies were piled in our back yard was never clear to me but the bodies were in a spot where the Vietnamese troops could not see them. I thought this was done so the morale of the Vietnamese troops would not be adversely affected by the event since many of these troops in our camp also had their wives and children living with them or in the nearby village. It was clear by the trauma on the bodies that violent explosions had torn up many of the bodies of soldiers, women and children. I still remember the body of one young Vietnamese female, who had her upper torso and head missing and a small baby with its upper torso also missing. I imagined that she was a young mother, clutching her baby in a shallow trench or fox hole when a strong blast in front of them sheared off her and the baby's upper torso. Death would have been mercifully instantaneous.

The pile of bodies sat in our camp for two days and when it began raining, we used our ponchos to cover the bodies. By the second day, the stench from the bodies was becoming unbearable. Vietnamese military trucks finally returned and removed the bodies to a burial site. The sight of dead soldiers in uniform was a more normal or expected sight but to see mutilated bodies of women and children caused by violent explosions was harder to view and not be deeply affected by it.

I never heard any explanation of why the Viet Cong targeted this particular camp to annihilate but it was located on the Cambodian border actively monitoring enemy troop movements in Cambodia which was only a few hundred meters away from their camp. A copy of the "situation report" that I filed on this incident is included as an insert.

Tet

On January 31, 1968, communist forces in Vietnam launched a well coordinated attack on dozens of targets throughout South Vietnam including our remote location in the Mekong delta. I remember the event well but I do not remember why several of us team members were away from our camp when the attack started. The result was that part of our team was mortared in Camp An Phu and although our camp took several direct hits, no one was injured and the buildings suffered little damage.

Meanwhile, the rest of our team including myself, spent the night of Tet on a Navy PBR boat, anchored in the middle of the Mekong River near Chau Doc. At first light, we proceeded to Chau Doc and joined our B team comrades. Most of the fighting and infiltration of enemy troops had occurred in the middle of the night. As dawn approached, contact was broken and the enemy troops retreated and disappeared in the Chau Doc area. Local intelligence sources reported that the Viet Cong troops had all carried civilian clothing with them when they entered the town. Once the attack was over and day light approached, they stashed their weapons, donned their civilian clothes and walked out of Chau Doc along with thousands of other fleeing civilians.

In downtown Chau Doc, there was a four story hotel that was rumored to be harboring some Viet Cong soldiers. My CO volunteered our team to secure the hotel. We started on the ground floor and went from room to room confirming that the hotel was vacant. If doors were locked, we would kick in the doors and enter the room with rifles pointed and ready to fire. After each floor was secured, we went to the next higher floor until we reached the roof which we also checked to ensure no enemy soldiers were hiding there. The hotel had at least 50 rooms. It was nerve wracking to kick in doors to enter rooms, with no clue as to what we would find; trapped civilians or enemy combatants with their rifles also ready to fire. If there had been enemy soldiers in the rooms, we would have fired at each other simultaneously from about 15 feet and shot or killed each other on the spot. Fortunately, the hotel was completely empty. Some American nurses were stranded at a nearby hospital and several Navy SEALS took a couple of jeeps and rescued them and brought them back to the B team compound.

Up until Tet, the American military press and some civilian press had presented an image of the war being won militarily and the communist forces were weakening. The Tet offensive changed the public perception that we were winning the war. It was clear that the communist forces had the ability to strike at will anywhere in the country. The enemy intent was not to capture and hold any targets but it was to demonstrate that they could over run almost any small unit and then withdraw before there was a massive American or Vietnamese military response.

I believed that the Tet offensive was the turning point for many Vietnamese and American civilians and military, especially the Vietnamese military. The message was clear. The enemy was not weakening but had the strength and organization to launch dozens of simultaneous attacks country wide. Militarily, the Viet Cong took great losses as the American and Vietnamese forces counter attacked and quickly reclaimed areas that the Viet Cong had temporarily occupied. The psychological impact of this offensive was tremendous and seemed to me to clearly be a turning point in the war.

CHAPTER 4

VIETNAMESE PEOPLE

Over one and a half years, I had ample opportunity to meet many Vietnamese people when we did our community action programs or traveled with Vietnamese soldiers by truck, boat or on foot on patrol. As a race of people, I thought they were some of the most beautiful people I have seen anywhere in the world including other parts of Asia. They were almost all slender and of medium height, with black hair and brown eyes, medium to light olive complexions with delicate facial features. The farmers in the country had darker, more wrinkled skin as a result of excessive sun exposure. The urban populace generally had a lighter and more delicate complexion. Country farmers generally wore black pajama type trousers and shirts and conical woven bamboo sun shade hats. Some urban Vietnamese women would wear their traditional "*ao dais*" (pronounced ow yies), which was a combination pants suit with a billowing skirt that had thigh high slits on each side. It was prim and proper yet had a sensual appeal at the same time. Many urban women also wore the conical sun shade hats. The more westernized young women would wear western style clothing and miniskirts that would rival any that might be seen back in America. The urban men generally wore dark colored slacks and a white shirt. School kids in the city wore uniforms, many of them consisting of blue slacks or dresses with white shirts or blouses.

In our village area and the more remote parts of our district, we and the Green Berets soldiers that preceded us, were the only Americans the village people had ever seen or met. The children were always thrilled to see American soldiers and they were shy but friendly. They were unspoiled and they did not beg or attempt to steal from us. Adult Vietnamese soldiers would sometimes want to hold our hands and walk with us as a sign of friendship. This always seemed strange and uncomfortable to us but we followed local customs and held hands with them so as not to offend them.

The urban children in Saigon were a whole different story. They would mob American soldiers for the purpose of begging for money or candy or to steal a watch or camera off of an unsuspecting GI. I lost a watch off my wrist once, complete with the leather strap and buckle, to one of the little urban street urchins in Saigon.

The Vietnamese people that we met in the country in our area of operation were either farmers or vendors. They were honest, hard working, reserved country people and I thought they were very similar to rural Navajos in aspects of their lifestyle and mannerisms. They would spread a table cloth on the floor and sit around the food to eat which was a traditional Navajo custom. They cared for their land and livestock in a manner similar to Navajos. The major difference was they grew rice with abundant water while we Navajos grew corn with precious little water.

Most rural Vietnamese homes in our area were built along the banks of rivers that frequently flooded so most homes were built on stilts, 3 to 8 feet above the ground. These houses were lightly constructed of wood, bamboo, and palm fronds. While these houses were well suited to sub tropical weather, they offered little protection when a firefight erupted and bullets started flying. For this reason, most families constructed a small trench shelter under their houses where they could take refuge in the event of a local firefight.

The urban Vietnamese were very different in their dress and attitude. The educated Vietnamese had government jobs with the Vietnamese government or with American contractors, both civilian and military. There were many Vietnamese and Chinese entrepreneurs. There was a district in Saigon called Cholon where many Chinese businesses were located. During the French colonial period, Saigon was known as the "Pearl of the Orient". By the 1960s, it had become a tarnished pearl but it was still a vibrant, international city that was bursting at the seams with people and non-stop activity.

Many country people were forced to relocate to the city because of the war. They had to hustle to survive to feed themselves or to feed their families if married. Many under educated Vietnamese men were vendors, laborers or offered taxi services via bicycle "cyclos", motorcycles or the ubiquitous blue and tan Renault taxicabs. Older women were generally street vendors. Younger women, particularly attractive women, were waitresses, clerks or hostesses and some worked part time or full time as prostitutes and made enormous amounts of money compared to regular hourly wage earners. The price of "quickie sex" in rural towns would range from 300 to 500 hundred Vietnamese piasters which was roughly the equivalent of $2.50 to $4.00 US dollars. In Saigon the price for sex, was triple or quadruple that of the rural areas. Many Vietnamese people resented the American soldiers for their loud boisterous behavior but loved them at the same time for their money which was freely spent. For many Vietnamese, uprooted by the war, their livelihood came from American soldiers or American jobs created by the war effort. This seems to be a universal problem. During WWII, the English people resented the American soldiers based in England. They had a saying that the problem with American soldiers was that they were "overpaid, over sexed and over here."

When I first arrived in Vietnam in late 1966, there were fewer rules and restrictions on American soldiers since the massive buildup of American troops had just begun. By the time I left Vietnam in 1968, there were all types of rules and regulations and a general militarization of the country and city of Saigon. I suppose it was necessary to maintain order with a large number of American troops in country but it was clearly a less enjoyable and more restrictive experience than my earlier days in Vietnam.

Co Xu

It was late spring of 1967 when I met a beautiful young school teacher in a nearby village. Our advisory team visited Vinh Loc village to assess the needs of the local school as part of our community development mission. Our advisory team visited the village with a reinforced squad of eight Vietnamese soldiers since this village was not the friendliest one in our district. Co Xu (pronounced coe sue) was the local primary school teacher in this village and lived with her parents in a nice bamboo house built on stilts near the bank of the Bassac River. She invited us three team members to her home for tea. I was the radio operator and attended the event with my XO, Captain Land, and a fellow sergeant. She spoke French and limited English and was the most beautiful and adorable lady I had met in Vietnam. As pleasantries were exchanged, Co Xu explained how her parents had valued education and sacrificed a lot for her to attend secondary school and college in Can Tho and Saigon.

"It is important to me to come home to teach young children in our village," she explained "I apologize that my English is not good but I want to more practice to get better," she carefully explained. She was charming as she searched for the correct English words to use. She appeared to be in her mid twenties and had the most beautiful face and expressive dark eyes.

Our Executive Officer explained that he wanted to help improve her school and requested a list of school supplies that would help in her teaching efforts. Co Xu promised to develop a list within a weeks' time. The Vietnamese counterpart to the American advisory team, Major Phan, had explained to us earlier that there was a strong Viet Cong infrastructure in Vinh Loc village. If we wanted to go there during daylight hours, we would need a reinforced squad for protection just in case the Viet Cong decided to get aggressive. Going there after dark was very dangerous and not possible without a major military presence.

It became apparent to me, that our XO had a personal interest in Co Xu and her school and he was committed to returning to the village to pick up the list of her desired school supplies. I accompanied our XO on his return trip to the village to pick up the supply list a week later. Tea was again served and Co Xu was a gracious host.

"Thank you very much for your generous effort to help our children get education" she told us.

Although our two meetings had been brief and formal, Co Xu and I made eye contact that meant more than just polite hospitality, in my mind. I replayed these two brief meetings in my mind to savor the nuances of her French accented English, her shy smile, her shiny black hair and olive complexion. I wanted to see her again in the worst way but it was impossible to go unaccompanied to Vinh Loc village.

Weeks went by and I did not see or communicate with Co Xu. I was not even certain there was anything to communicate with her about but her eyes told me there was. I wondered if my feelings were just the product of an overactive imagination of a 21 year old, lonely soldier, half a world away from home in America.

Due partly to the efforts of our XO, a reception and dinner was planned for the An Phu District Chief. He invited two dozen prominent citizens from nearby district villages to attend. Co Xu and her parents were among the invitees. I was ecstatic upon learning that she would be attending the dinner in one weeks time.

Finally, the big day arrived. After numerous toasts and a sumptuous dinner of chicken, fish and shrimp there was a social mixing of the Vietnamese civilians and American soldiers. This was my first chance to speak with Co Xu in a semi private manner.

"Chao Co, Mon yoi?" (Hello Miss, how are you?), I greeted her.

"You speak Vietnamese very good," she responded. "You are a handsome man and should be an ambassador."

"You are a most gracious lady, thank you." I responded carefully, barely maintaining my composure. The dinner party was wonderful and my limited conversation with Co Xu was enthralling. I was a Native American with an olive complexion and many people had commented that I looked like a tall Vietnamese soldier. Prior to meeting Co Xu, I had not met any Vietnamese woman that had attracted me in the manner that Co Xu did. In my wildest fantasies, I wanted to profess my enchantment for her but I knew this was not realistic. Any respectable Vietnamese woman would not consider being seen in public with an American soldier, especially an enlisted man. If a Vietnamese woman were seen in public with an American soldier, the presumption of Vietnamese people would be that she was either a prostitute, or at best, a mistress to the soldier.

Two months went by with no communication between myself and Co Xu and then one morning, Co Xu arrived at our camp in An Phu and entered our teams living room area.

"Please, I want to see Captain Land" she wailed as she cried openly with frequent sobs.

When Captain Land appeared, she blurted out, "Captain Land, will you marry me and take me to America? My parents have arranged for me to marry a Vietnamese Army Officer that I barely know and do not love. I know it is hard for a Vietnamese to go to America but you are American officer and can get approval." she pleaded. Her eyes were red and she continued to cry openly.

Captain Land tried to placate Co Xu, "I would like to take you to America but I cannot get approval for you to go," he explained trying to remain calm.

"Why can you not take me there? You like me and I can marry you and then I can go to America with you. You are American officer," she responded, still crying.

"There is too much paperwork and I cannot get approval in time for you to go," he explained patiently, although he was clearly embarrassed about this public discussion within earshot of a half dozen team members. The XO continued to try to explain why Army regulations would not allow him to take her to America without a lot of time consuming paperwork with little chance of success even for an American officer. The XO was due to rotate home to America within two months time.

"I thought you liked me and it was my hope to know you more in the future, but you do not want me to go with you. You are not a good man," she sobbed, as she turned and ran from the room and down the path away from our camp.

The awkward silence lingered as the nearby team members quietly drifted away from the vicinity and pretended that they had not really heard every word of this intense encounter.

I felt so sad for Co Xu. I knew that this was the act of a desperate woman who had no options left and had swallowed all her pride in a desperate last attempt to avoid a forced marriage. I hoped that the XO would reconsider and agree to take her to America but I knew he was already engaged to be married. As a young enlisted man that had barely become an E-4 specialist, a few months before, I knew I could never get military approval to take a Vietnamese woman home and despite the mutual attraction I imagined we had, I was unsure if she would break a Vietnamese social taboo and marry an enlisted man of lower social status than an officer.

I never saw nor heard of Co Xu again and have often wondered what happened to her.

Epicurean delights

Our advisory team worked closely with the local Vietnamese military units as well as the local elected public officials. In an advisory role, we met and ate with the Vietnamese frequently. Many excellent meals were shared consisting of rice, chicken and fish. Occasionally some of the foods offered were exotic by American standards but I never refused any food offered to me although there were a few times that I ate sparingly and drank a lot of beer.

In my family home, my Navajo mother came from a sheep raising family and my Seminole father came from a cattle raising family. As children, our family ate every part of the sheep and cow and I was accustomed to different types of food that others people might consider exotic. It was the advisory team's belief, verified by Vietnamese themselves, that they would eat anything that moved. It was not unusual to be on a combat patrol and see a Vietnamese soldier with a dead snake tied to his belt. The snake was destined for the evening dinner pot usually prepared as a stew. At one time, the advisory team had a pet boa constrictor snake for several months that mysteriously disappeared. The snake was about four feet long so it must have made a huge meal for some Vietnamese soldiers.

Another delicacy was dog; preferably a young, black, male puppy. There was one memorable meal I shared with the Vietnamese artillery crew that was located in our camp. The Vietnamese had acquired a young black male puppy and they invited our advisory team members to join them for dinner. Our interpreter and myself accepted the invitation while other team members declined. A fire was built and maintained by dribbling in gun powder pellets from a bag that was the propellant charge for the 155 mm howitzer. The puppy meat was cubed and then seared and sautéed in a sauce and served along with rice and vegetable dishes. The meal was good and the camaraderie was great. Many of the Vietnamese meat dishes were sautéed or cooked in a stew and were indistinguishable from one another and the standard joke when describing strange food was that it "tasted like chicken."

One Sunday afternoon, a Vietnamese Captain told us that he and some of his men were going out to hunt bats and we were invited to a bat feast later in the evening. The Captain and several soldiers left camp in two jeeps and returned several hours later with the backs of the jeeps filled with bats. These were not regular bats but were monster fruit bats that had six feet wing spans and the body resembled a small, furry red fox. After much butchering, cleaning and cooking, we were invited to a bat meal. The bat soup was delicious but the fried bat meat was dark and tough and not particularly tasty.

During our meal, I asked one of the Vietnamese soldiers how they hunted the bats and through our interpreter, he told me that they would go into a region that had tall trees typically used by fruit bats to nest in during the day. They would ask local farmers if they had seen any bats in the area. Once they had an affirmative answer, they would scrutinize the trees and proceed to spray likely tree tops with automatic sub machine gun fire. If a tree had fruit bats nesting in them, they would start dropping out of the trees (like dead bats).

Our advisory team had a Vietnamese interpreter that lived with us as a team member. He was a city boy from Saigon who had been conscripted into the Vietnamese army. He hated serving in the Vietnamese Army and he missed his family terribly. He spoke excellent English and French and was our principle communication link with many Vietnamese. Many of the Vietnamese officers spoke good French and a little English so team members could usually converse with them.

Private Thien and I became good friends and a bet was wagered that I could eat anything Pvt. Thien could eat. Pvt. Thien would win the bet if he brought some food back to camp that he would eat in my presence and that I would refuse to eat. He took this as a personal challenge and would go looking for unusual food items to bring back to test me. A couple of the more unusual items he brought back were eggs that he called "100 year old Chinese eggs". These eggs had been buried underground for an unknown time period and had turned dark gray with a pungent, creamy, sulfurous smelling core which had previously been the egg yolk. Pvt. Thien could barely eat his egg and gagged as he finished it. I ate my egg cautiously and we were both thankful that we only had one egg each to eat.

Another memorable discovery by Pvt Thien was fertilized, aged, chicken eggs containing the intact embryos. These were eaten by poking a hole in the end of the egg and picking out pieces with chopsticks. Pvt. Thien and I had both agreed to eat these eggs with a lot of beer which helped everything go down easier. I explained to my teammates later that it had a strong egg smell and tasted okay, but not much chicken taste at all. My only complaint was that the embryo beak would get stuck between my teeth and had to be picked out with a toothpick (said in jest). This elicited a series of groans from my American team members.

Vietnamese farmers were very resourceful and masters of recycling, including human waste. In our region of Vietnam, many farmers had either, fish ponds or floating fish cages along the river banks, These ponds and cages had a toilet fitted over them and the toilet assembly would be a few feet above the water. When people used these toilets, the water would start frothing with fish fighting for the solid feces that hit the water. These fish were raised and eaten by the family and sold in the local markets. We naturally called these "shit fish" and instructed our maids to only buy fish that were caught in the rivers. We liked to believe that all of the fish that we ate were "free range" river fish and not shit fish but we were never quite sure.

The Vietnamese country cuisine was a delicious mixture of Vietnamese, Chinese, and French influences. Our local village of An Phu had a population of approximately 4,000 people and had an amazing variety of goods and services available. There was a small market with fresh produce, a meat market offering primarily chicken and fish and occasionally water buffalo. There was also a small bakery, a photography shop, a garage and metal working shop. We did not have access to Army food or rations so we were given a cost of living allowance (COLA) in order to buy our food off the local economy. We pooled our money to purchase local food as previously mentioned. The other option was to send team members to large military installations in Can Tho or Saigon, to buy fresh American food at military post exchanges (PX).

Our team primarily ate chicken and fish but would crave red meat occasionally. When this happened, we instructed our maids to find some beef or oxen meat. On one occasion they brought back some water buffalo meat that was the toughest meat anyone on our team had ever attempted to eat. After grilling it, the team sat down to eat their meal with mini loaves of bread, rice and vegetables. The team knew the water buffalo would be leathery but no one anticipated just how chewy it would be. The thought was that tough red meat was better than no red meat at all. The meat was flavorful and team members chewed and chewed but could not break the meat down to swallowing size. Some members took the meat out of their mouths and put it back on their plate to let their jaws rest before attacking it again. The best method seemed to be to cut the meat into tiny pieces and chew it vigorously until the jaw became tired and then swallow the smaller pieces.

The local An Phu bakery made mini loaves of French bread specifically for us. These loaves were about 6 inches long and were a welcome change from the rice we normally ate. They had a few tiny black specks in them which were actually baked in bugs. A few bugs were tolerable and the rationale was that they were baked and dead and sterilized by the heat. The joke was that our bread was protein-fortified. Our CO was tolerant of a few bugs in our bread as we all were. But over time, the bugs in the bread would become more numerous to the point where there were dozens of dark bug specks in each mini loaf. Getting fed up with the excessive bugs, our CO would become irate and storm down to the local bakery with the interpreter and a bug laden loaf as an example. After a thorough discussion about our health and the need to have proper nutrition and bug free bread, our CO would return, much relieved that he had educated the local baker about sanitation measures. For a few weeks, the bread would be almost bug free but gradually, more and more bugs would again be found in our bread. This would eventually prompt another visit by our CO to the local bakery and the cycle would repeat itself.

One of my more memorable river trips was made via a Vietnamese landing craft boat (LCVP), from Chau Doc to Can Tho. This trip was made over several days so that our team could purchase some American food supplies from the Can Tho PX. The trip took one day downstream on the Bassac river and 2 or 3 days returning upstream.

One hot day, our boat stopped by a local riverside village so the boat crew and ourselves could get something to eat and drink. The cost of a bottle of beer was about one half bottle deposit and one half beer contents. The Vietnamese soldiers wanted to treat us so they emptied a .50 caliber ammo can and filled it half full of ice. They then bought a case of beer and emptied all the beer into the ammo can and left the bottles with the merchant to avoid the cost of the bottle deposit. The sincerity of the Vietnamese troops was touching since we Americans were paid so much better than our Vietnamese counterparts. They insisted upon treating us to ice cold beer on the hot Bassac River and the camaraderie of the Vietnamese boat crew was truly memorable. While drinking beer, one Vietnamese soldier told me through our interpreter that he thought all soldiers around the world were the same. He said we all wanted to eat fast, drink fast and have sex often since we never knew when we would have our last meal and be killed.

Nouc mam (fish sauce) and rice wine were other staples of our diet when we traveled or dined with Vietnamese soldiers. Nouc mam was a fish sauce that was used as a flavoring much like soy sauce is used by the Chinese on their food. This sauce was used on many foods and was available at every meal. Good quality nouc mam was refined and smooth tasting and enhanced the flavor of many foods. Poor quality nouc mam was available in the very rural areas and often homemade under very crude conditions and tasted like rancid fish sauce (which it was) and was to be avoided if at all possible.

Rice wine was another readily available commodity and was usually available at most meals along with beer. Good quality rice wine was similar to sake that the Japanese drank. Poor quality, local brew rice wine had the taste of rubbing alcohol and when mixed with tablespoons of raw sugar was often enough to guarantee that one or more team members would need to leave the room immediately after drinking and hurl the contents outside at their stomach's insistence. Beer was always a safe bet. It was consistent in quality, fairly cheap and readily available and far safer than drinking local water. The favorite Vietnamese beer was called "33" or *bah muy bah*. *San Miguel* beer from the Philippines was another favorite but it was expensive.

Vung Tau dinner

Upon arriving in the seaside resort of Vung Tau, I checked into an elegant, old french colonial style hotel with red clay roof tiles, thick masonry walls and high ceilings. Hotel staff informed me it was mandatory that all weapons be checked in while on leave in Vung Tau. I figured this rule had to do with the old adage that alcohol and gun powder did not mix. In our district, team members always carried their rifles and, when traveling, a .45 caliber pistol was carried concealed in a shoulder holster under our army fatigues. I reluctantly turned in my pistol since the penalties for getting caught with a weapon in Vung Tau were severe. I was assured that Vung Tau was safe and weapons were not needed since there were adequate armed MPs (military police) present to ensure security but I still felt naked and vulnerable without my weapon.

During most of my first year in Vietnam, I was the only radio operator our team had so I was always on duty, 24/7. During my second year, our team finally received a second radio operator and after training him, I applied to take a three day, in-country leave to Vung Tau which was a seaside resort on the east coast of Vietnam. My CO approved my leave request and I was on my way, hitching rides by boat and helicopter.

My first day of leave was dedicated to checking out the US Army Enlisted Men's (EM) bars and local Vietnamese night clubs. The main attraction of the EM bars was cheap booze; beer was ten cents a can and mixed drinks were 25 cents. The main distractions of these bars were the absence of females and young soldiers learning how to drink, usually drunk and noisy. The floors would be sloshing with spilled beer and cigarette butts.

The local Vietnamese night clubs main distractions were the expensive prices for watered down drinks and more drunk soldiers. The main attractions were young, beautiful, and available Vietnamese girls. This outweighed all the other distractions. One of these young lovelies became my "date" for the night or at least for a couple of hours. My date was young and beautiful and for a negotiated price, she took me to her apartment for a sexual encounter. This was obviously enjoyable, but afterwards back in my hotel room, I felt alone and lonely. It was difficult going to sleep after my alcohol buzz wore off. I had been away from home for over a year and I missed my family, friends, and the reservation. I finally drifted off to sleep, thinking about home.

Awakening on the second day of leave, I felt emotionally empty and lonely for home or a family connection. The previous night had been fun and physically satisfying but, strictly a business transaction with no emotional significance. Not looking for a repeat of the night before, I went to the seaside and enjoyed the white sandy beaches of the South

China sea and the gentle ocean waves. The waters were warm and soothing to my body.

The mostly empty beaches featured young, beautiful, bikini clad girls with inviting, "come on" smiles. The beauty and tranquility of Vung Tau seemed to be of another country, far removed from the ugliness of the war devouring this country.

While getting lunch and a beer at midday, I met a friendly waitress that spoke decent English.

While not as beautiful as the bar girls of the night before, she was attractive and had a wholesome quality about her that appealed to me. She was slender, of medium height, with long black hair and a warm, natural smile. Although not explicitly stated, I understood that Co Mai could be available for the evening. I had several beers and since it was early afternoon and the restaurant bar was quiet, I talked with Co Mai at length.

Co Mai was in her mid twenties, widowed, and originally from a small farming village about 20 kilometers(12 miles) west of Vung Tau. She came from a farming family but due to the war, they could not farm, and they now lived on the outskirts of Vung Tau. Her parents sold vegetables as street vendors. She worked as a waitress becoming the principal breadwinner for her family which also included her young child and a younger brother and sister. She didn't complain but it was clear that life was tough for her family. Young Vietnamese women sold their bodies to support their children and extended families. It was a pragmatic decision made under war time conditions with very few options available to uneducated, displaced country women.

Talking with Co Mai, I learned that she got off work at 4 PM.

"Co Mai, I would like to have dinner with you and your family tonight. I will buy all the food and you and your family can make dinner and we can eat together as friends. I want you to be my friend. You do not have to sleep with me. Just friends. Understand?"

Co Mai looked at me quizzically and then a big smile spread across her face.

"Okay, number one! You pay me and we have big dinner with my family?"

"Yes, this is what I want to do. Okay?"

"Okay, Okay." she smiled.

We worked out the details and I told her what I liked to eat. She gave me a note with an address where she would meet me later. I gave her 2,000 piasters (16 US dollars) and told her I would meet her at the agreed upon time. I then left the restaurant and went back to my hotel room to relax and clean up for my "dinner date." I was fully aware that I could be getting ripped off but I did not believe Co Mai would do that. She was an honest country girl and not one of the Saigon hustlers who specialized in ripping off naive GIs. After almost a year in Vietnam, I had learned some expensive lessons from the Saigon bar hustlers.

Leaving my hotel at 6 PM, I caught a three wheeled bicycle "cyclo", with a seat attached to the front for the passengers. I gave the address to the cyclo man, and settled into the front facing "suicide seat" for a leisurely ride to the outskirts of Vung Tau. At the appointed place, Co Mai met me and we walked down an alley to her house.

"Please understand" she explained, "my family is now poor because of the war and our house is not good. We had a nice house when we lived on our farm."

"Do not worry. I live in a small house in America also. I understand." I tried to put her at ease. After about one block down the alley street, we came to Co Mai's house.

"Please come in Trung si," (sergeant), she said in a formal manner.

The house, or hut, was made primarily from bamboo and corrugated sheet metal. The floor was hard packed dirt and lit by kerosene lamps. Some houses on the Navajo reservation were built in a similar manner (without the bamboo). The tiny living room also served as the dining room and Co Mai's family was sitting on the floor around a plastic table cloth laden with food. Introductions were made all around and I sat down with the family on the floor.

Co Mai's mother and father were in their mid forties while her brother and sister were still in their mid teens. Co Mai's beautiful baby boy was about three years old with coal black hair and bright eyes. The family was very reserved but cordial and genuinely friendly to me whom they must have regarded as a strange American who looked like them and sat on the floor with them to eat dinner. The dinner consisted of *tit ga* (chicken), *ca* (fish), *nuoc mam* (fish sauce), spring rolls with shrimp, mini-loaves of French bread, noodles, rice and vegetables. The platters of food were set in the middle of the table cloth and everyone dished out their portions onto their plates and bowls. I was very proficient with chop sticks by now and used them as easily as I would use a fork back home.

Co Mai's family repeated what Co Mai had already related to me regarding her family. Because of the war, they had to leave their farm and move to a safer place. Co Mai's husband was a soldier but he died a couple of years earlier. They had the highest praise for what Co Mai did for the family and she appeared to be the major breadwinner (rice winner?) for the family unit. I was struck by the apparent lack of bitterness this family had for their terrible situation. They accepted their circumstances as a part of their life during war time. They planned to return to their village once the war was over. This was not the first war they had experienced, since the French and the Japanese had occupied Vietnam in the 1940s and 50s. I wondered how most American families would cope with life if they were placed in similar circumstances.

They were honored to be eating dinner with an American and kept apologizing for the lack of amenities they would have provided if they were back home on their farm. I tried to put them at ease. They had many questions of me and were unclear of the concept of an American Indian. They were familiar with the term of an Indian from India but not an American Indian or Native American. Nearly all Vietnamese had seen cowboy and Indian movies before and they identified the Indians as Viet Cong and the cowboys and cavalry as the US Army. Reluctantly, I used this analogy and explained that American Indians lived in America first. Then the white people came from Europe and fought with the Native Americans but that was over 100 years ago. The US Army and white men no longer fought the American Indians. Native Americans like me, joined the US Army to help the Vietnamese in their fight against the communists.

As the dinner progressed, the family became much more open and the conversation more lively using Co Mai as the interpreter. The family asked many questions about life in America and it became clear to me that this family, other than Co Mai, had never had a chance to have an extended conversation with an American, much less a brown skinned American Indian sitting down to dinner with them.

Everyone had their fill of the delicious dinner with food left over. After a couple of hours of conversation, I told the family I had to return to my hotel due to a curfew for American soldiers. I thanked the family for their hospitality, wonderful dinner and conversation. The Vietnamese family thanked me also and after the goodbyes were completed, Co Mai escorted me back down the alley to the main street. I shook Co Mai's hand and thanked her and bid her goodbye. I then caught another bicycle "cyclo" back to my hotel.

I went to bed that night, happy and fulfilled in an emotional sense. I felt like I had just had an exotic picnic dinner with some of my relatives back on the Navajo reservation.

The next day was the end of my leave and the dinner with Co Mai and her family was the highlight of my Vung Tau R & R.

CHAPTER 5

EXTENSION AND EUROPE

S ince childhood, I had wanted to travel and see the world, especially Europe. My twelve month Vietnam tour would end in October, 1967. I would then return to a stateside Army base and sit around for six months and endure Mickey Mouse regulations until I was discharged when my two year enlistment ended. The normal tour of duty for Army personnel in Vietnam was twelve months. As an incentive to retain experienced soldiers in Vietnam, the Army offered a bonus for soldiers that would extend for an additional six months in Vietnam. For this six month extension, a soldier could travel anywhere they wanted in the free world on a 30 day paid leave.

My plan was to extend for six months and go to Europe for 30 days. I would also stop off at home in America on my way to and from Europe. My 30 days in Europe would not start until I arrived at my chosen destination. Some of my Special Forces buddies had done this so this became my plan. I picked London, England, as my destination and I also applied for a transfer to a MACV reconnaissance unit which did reconnaissance in enemy territory in small teams for 4 or 5 men for my final six months of duty. This sounded interesting to me and I felt better knowing I would be kept busy for my entire two year enlistment. I would then leave Vietnam in April, 1968, and be discharged as soon as I returned to America.

This was my plan, but when I got to Saigon to pick up my flight tickets, the Army had changed its' policy. Instead of sending me on an easterly route through America to London, England, I was sent on a westerly route directly to London, England, non-stop, with refueling stops in Cambodia, Thailand, India, Iran, Lebanon, Turkey, Yugoslavia, Germany and finally, England. This destroyed my entire plan to get home to visit family and friends but I still preferred to finish out my army enlistment doing something interesting. Hopefully my extension would be worthwhile even though I had my doubts. I accepted my new flight plan and departed from Tan Son Nhut air base on a TWA flight bound for Phnom Penh, Cambodia, on October 5, 1967. Phnom Penh, was only about eighty miles from where I was stationed in An Phu. We were not allowed to deplane in Phnom Penh, but I saw several MIG fighter jets on the tarmac. Cambodia was officially a neutral country but everyone knew that it was a safe haven for North Vietnamese regular troops and South Vietnamese communist guerillas. I was relieved when we left Phnom Penh. It had an oppressive atmosphere much like being in a hostile or enemy country.

We stopped next in Bangkok, Thailand where we had an eight hour layover. I left the airport and toured the city with a couple of young Thai guides who drove me around in a 1957

Chevrolet in pristine condition. They were very friendly and fluent in English and showed me as much as they could of the modern city in four hours before returning me to the airport.

While waiting for the continuation flight, I met a young American hippy type guy with a back pack who was traveling the world. During our wide ranging conversation, he asked me what my religion was and I told him I had none in the Christian sense of the word. He corrected me and said everyone has a religion, even it is a religion of one person. This impressed me and I recounted to him how I had told a sergeant during my initial enlistment period to put "no preference" on my army identification tag (i.e, dog tag). The sergeant became angry with me and told me that when I was in a foxhole in Vietnam getting shot at, that I would change my mind and find a religion. This hippy was also strongly opposed to the war in Vietnam and this was the first of many conversations I would have with people in Europe concerning the war. It marked the acceleration of the change in my attitude toward the war which I had unquestioningly accepted before going to Vietnam. I had serious doubts about what we were doing in Vietnam after I was there for most of a year. Upon leaving Vietnam and talking with civilians in Europe I became more aware of my own developing reservations toward the war.

We flew next to India, landing in New Delhi. This leg of the trip was memorable for me, when I finally realized that the clouds I saw to the north of our flight pattern were not clouds at all but the snow capped Himalayan mountain range which peak out at about 29,000 feet which was the approximate cruise altitude of our Boeing 707 airliner. The poverty in New Delhi was evident, even at the airport and was depressing. After New Delhi, our flight became the local commuter route for that part of the world. We stopped in Teheran, Iran – Beirut, Lebanon – Istanbul, Turkey – Belgrade, Yugoslavia – Frankfurt, Germany and finally London, England. Since we gained one hour as we flew west into different time zones, I gained approximately ten hours time and my body clock as well as my wristwatch were totally confused by the time I arrived in London, England. My official travel orders authorized me to visit the American Embassy in London. After 30 days, I was to depart England and return to my duty station in Vietnam.

I left Vietnam in a short sleeve shirt in hot tropical weather and I arrived in London a day later, in cool, drizzly weather that did not improve over the several days that I stayed there. London was a very civilized city. The taxicab drivers wore dark three piece suits and the people were friendly and polite. I loved the English breakfasts with sausage, eggs, thin white toast and generous dollops of orange marmalade, which is still my favorite jam today. Those breakfasts and fish and chips stand out in my mind as the only remarkable British cuisine I experienced. The first few times, I spoke on a telephone, I used army radio protocol such as "Roger" and to terminate a conversation, I used the word, "out." I felt foolish doing this and was thankful I was not talking directly to someone using my radio terminology. After a few days, I started talking normally and began feeling more normal amongst all the Anglo- Saxon population in a peacetime setting. My plan when I got to Europe was to see the maximum amount possible in 30 days or until I spent the $1,000 I had with me. In my freshman year of college, I had taken introductory courses in architecture, art and humanities. European artists and architecture were prominent in western civilization so I had definite ideas on what I wanted to see.

After five days in London, I had seen the city sights and more importantly, I had re-civilized myself and relaxed and grown accustomed to large numbers of Anglo Saxon civilians in a busy peaceful city. The English police, "bobbies," carried a baton and no firearms which I thought was so strange. London still bore signs of WWII damage with scarred buildings which had been damaged by shrapnel from the bombing blitz of London at the beginning of WWII in 1940. The museums in London were excellent and the British Museum had a comprehensive Egyptian antiquities exhibit. Egypt was a former colony of England so the English had ample opportunity to expropriate many foreign cultural treasures.

Munich, Germany was a vibrant city with brisk, clear weather. My plan was to attend the Munich Oktoberfest, beer festival, but I was one week late and missed it. The streets were busy and the German food had character with a lot of beef and pork dishes, sausages and pastries. I thought it was amazing that you could buy these delicious snack foods and beer on the street. As a people, the southern Germans seemed more friendly and relaxed to me than their northern countrymen. I went to a world famous beer hall, the "*Hofbrauhaus* ", one night for a meal and a beer. The building had three levels. The ground floor was a beer hall. The second level served casual family dinners and the third level hosted formal dining and special events. I ate and drank in the beer hall on the ground floor. The men in the beer hall would periodically break out in German beer drinking songs. I visited with an older man that had been in WWII on the eastern front fighting the Russians. He said it was very hard duty there and he had been cold for the entire duration he was there and felt lucky to have lived through it. In talking about WWII he said the northern

Germans wanted the war and southern Germans basically just went along, but the entire country suffered the consequences.

I visited Dachau which was referred to by our tour guide as the *kremitorium*, (crematorium). The smokestacks and ovens were still there along with the custom made steel litter baskets. These baskets were used to insert dead bodies into the ovens to incinerate the remains. There was one barrack left standing. All the dozens of other barracks had been razed. A museum documented some of the atrocities committed by the Nazis. I had previously read of the holocaust so I knew some of the history but to actually be in a concentration camp and see firsthand the buildings and ovens was a startling reality for me. I found it hard to comprehend how "civilized" human beings could treat one another in such a barbaric manner. I still do not understand how an entire population could passively allow the holocaust to happen.

After Germany, I toured France and spent time in Paris and Nice. Paris is a beautiful city and the art and architecture overwhelming in its grandeur and plentitude. The Louvre Museum has to be one of the best museums in the world, if not the best. The night life was non-stop and the cabarets and floor shows were lavish and sensual. Nice was a beautiful, quiet seaside city since the summer vacation and tourist season was over by mid October. It was very peaceful and relaxing. I ordered beef *tartare* one night hoping to get something similar to a hamburger but what I got was seasoned raw ground beef. I ate it reluctantly and permanently added another word to my limited French vocabulary.

I took a bus tour to Monaco and tried my luck at the Monte Carlo casino with little success. When leaving Monte Carlo, our tour bus would not start so about twenty of us passengers got out and pushed our bus to get it started for our return to Nice. High rollers we were not. From France, I went to Italy and visited Florence, Rome and Naples. I was impressed with the gold jewelry stops in Florence. In Rome, the water fountains, Coliseum, Pantheon and the catacombs were memorable in addition to the rich historic ambiance of the entire city. The Romans were skilled and organized architects and builders and their structures have endured for over two millennium. From Rome, I went to Naples and toured the volcano, Vesuvius, which was still active. Nearby Pompei was a retirement community for Roman bureaucrats and soldiers. In 79 AD, it was buried by volcanic ash from Vesuvius and frozen in time until unearthed in the 19th century. The small village looked as if it were abandoned only a month earlier.. There were ruts in the stone paved streets, plumbing systems for running water and public bath houses. Ceramic tiles depicted everyday life scenes in ancient Italy as well as oriental scenes which indicated trade routes with far eastern Asia were well established 2000 years ago. People were buried on the streets of Pompei in volcanic ash and when the city was unearthed, plaster was poured into the cavities made by the fallen bodies. These plaster casts recreate the terror of these unfortunate people with frozen facial expressions.

From Naples, I started traveling back toward England for my return to Vietnam. I stopped in Amsterdam for a few days. I found the people there to be some of the friendliest in Europe. Many of them spoke English and I thought their beer was the best in Europe, challenged only by German brews. Holland was a very progressive country and prostitution was legal and confined to a specific section of Amsterdam. There were about two city blocks where women would sit in shop windows and advertise their merchandise which were themselves. Some would wear exotic clothing, while others would wear sportswear, or black leather tights. If interested, customers entered the shops, discussed prices, and if there was agreement, the shop would close temporarily. Men and women from around the world would stroll the streets, window shopping.

One of the sites I visited in Amsterdam was the hiding place of the Otto Frank Jewish family. Otto Frank had a daughter named Anne Frank whose diary immortalized the plight of many Jews trying to survive the German holocaust of WWII. The upstairs room where they hid seemed to have been left untouched since the family was discovered and shipped off to concentration camps in mid 1944. All the clothing and personal effects were gone but the writing and newspapers articles were still plastered on the walls of their hideout. There was a strong sense of sadness in those rooms since everyone knew who had lived and hidden there and their sad fate.

The Frank family lived in their hideout for two years and almost survived the war. Unfortunately, they were discovered and sent to concentration camps. Anne Frank died of disease in the Bergen Belsen concentration camp in Poland in early March of 1945, just weeks before the camp was liberated in April of 1945. She was 15 years old when she died. Her memory and spirit lives on in her diary and in numerous plays and movies about her life. The world should become a better place by the fact that her diary was discovered and became a worldwide reminder of what should never happen again.

After touring the Netherlands, I returned to London. I had enjoyed my tour of Europe and saw many sights that I had only dreamed of seeing as a child but it was also one of the loneliest times in my life since I would sometimes go for days and only speak a few words of English to a fellow American or a European that knew English. I treasured the conversations I did have.

I then began my easterly journey back to Vietnam for my six month extension of duty. It was during the period when I was in Europe that I began to mentally sort out my feelings and perceptions of the war in Vietnam and the American involvement. There is no one precise moment in Vietnam during my first twelve months there that I had an epiphany regarding whether America should be involved in Vietnam. The loss of civilian life was always tragic, especially if they were children. We did our "walks in the sun" which was essentially a hike to keep us busy. The Vietnamese that organized these missions seemed to know that there would be no enemy contact. I could see the psychological advantage that the VC had over the South Vietnamese troops. Most of South Vietnamese troops had little motivation to fight and the Viet Cong had them "psyched" out. Many Vietnamese seemed to strive only to survive the war and then they would resume a more normal life. It did not seem to matter much who won the war, just that there be peace and that they would be alive to enjoy it.

For us Americans who went to Vietnam for one year tours, we expected to make a big difference in one year and we expected the Vietnamese to act with the same sense of urgency that we did. It didn't happen. Many Vietnamese had experienced war their entire lives dating back to the Japanese occupation during WWII in the early 1940s.

I met some American draft dodgers in Amsterdam who were intensely interested in me when they found out that I was stationed in Vietnam. They urged me to dessert and leave the US Army. My sense of duty prevented me from considering this option, but the arguments they made were thought provoking. I remember a discussion I had with an American civilian passenger on one of these tours. This man wanted to know my perceptions of how the Vietnam war was being conducted and the American chances of success. I responded that if we switched sides, we could win the war in one day and the end result would be the same as if we stayed there many more years. My answer surprised even me but this was how I felt at that point in time.

While I was in Vietnam at Camp An Phu, we rarely discussed the merits of the war and whether we should be involved. The fact of the matter was that we were involved and we were there as soldiers of the United States of America. We accepted US policy and were there to do our jobs for one year. We would then go home and resume our civilian lives or go to other Army assignments elsewhere in the world, preferably back in America. Our news of the outside world and growing dissent in America was very limited. We had the armed forces radio station which was there for military morale building and entertainment. We received occasional copies of the "Stars and Stripes" newspaper which was primarily military news and entertainment. We had no television or direct link with the outside world unless we received weeks old American newspapers from home or we listened to short wave radio news reports from sources such as the British Broadcasting Corporation (BBC).

My first direct exposure to outside dissention to the Vietnam war occurred when I took a one week vacation, known as R&R, to Tokyo, Japan in May, 1967. I spent a five day vacation in Tokyo and met several bar hostesses that were educated and very fluent in English and were not afraid to express their opinions of Americans and our involvement in Vietnam. There was a strong anti-American sentiment among the young Japanese I met as well as very strong opposition to American involvement in Vietnam. This was in 1967 and WWII had ended just twenty- two years earlier with the dropping of two atomic bombs on Japan. I could understand their hostility to America and our military which still had bases on Japanese soil. It was during this R&R that I met another Navajo soldier in downtown Tokyo that was also on R&R from Vietnam. He was from Shiprock, NM, and we had a good visit, but unfortunately, I cannot remember his name.

CHAPTER 6

HOMEWARD BOUND

Upon returning from Europe, I had become more critical about American involvement in the war. I just wanted to finish out my six month extension, return home and get on with my civilian life and school. My request for transfer to a reconnaissance unit had been denied or totally ignored and I went back to my old unit in An Phu. Unfortunately, the last six months went by very slowly and I was not a happy camper. All of our team members had rotated home over the past year and I became the only original team member left from when I had first arrived in Camp An Phu. I remember being chastised by our third Commanding Officer and being counseled by a kindly First Sergeant that remarked how my attitude had changed. He encouraged me to be professional and have a positive attitude and finish out my tour in a good way. I took his words to heart and tried to think positive thoughts about my situation although it was a hard six months to endure. Most soldiers became more cautious as their tour neared completion and they got "short". Soldiers would want to stay behind in camp rather than go on combat missions but we really had no choice. If we were told to go on a mission, we went on a mission. This happened to me during my last week in Vietnam.

In mid April, 1968, we received reports of renewed enemy activity in Khan Binh, which was a hostile free fire zone in the north end of our sector of operation. We accompanied a Vietnamese company of RF soldiers on an assault of some new Viet Cong fortifications in this region. After meeting unexpected stiff resistance, we pulled back and waited for air support to soften up the target area. We withdrew about ¼ mile from the enemy positions and after about 30 minutes, some AE 1 "Skyraider" fighter bombers, arrived and dive bombed the enemy positions, dropping 500 pound bombs. We could see the bombs being released from the prop driven "Skyraiders". I was sitting down with my back against a tree and my legs spread out relaxing before our next assault. Suddenly, between my feet, a fist sized chunk of jagged metal landed after falling through the trees leaves from the sky. I leaned forward to pick it up but quickly dropped it because it was extremely hot. It was a fragment off of a 500 pound bomb that had just exploded seconds before and had missed hitting me by less than a foot. I felt blessed to not be hurt and that day was my last day in the field, during my last week, in Vietnam.

I don't remember much about leaving camp An Phu, other than packing my duffel bag with all my worldly possessions and leaving camp by boat and catching a helicopter ride from Chau Doc to Saigon where I processed out of Vietnam through Koelper Compound. We left all of our clothes and equipment and rifles in Vietnam. I wore an Army dress khaki uniform for travel. As we processed through Camp Alpha at Tan Son Nhut airport, getting ready to board the "big silver bird" for home, we passed a group of young soldiers who were just arriving in country. I felt so sorry for them and what they were about to experience over the next year and so happy for myself to be going home.

The flight home on the commercial 707 airliner was uneventful. We refueled in Manila, Philippines and in Honolulu, Hawaii before arriving in California, landing at Travis Air Force base. We were bussed to Oakland and I processed out of the Army the same day, April 25, 1968. There was a recruiter who gave us a half hearted pitch to re-enlist in the Army but he was greeted with jeers and not taken seriously by any soldiers. We only wanted to get out of the Army and go home. There was no such thing as post deployment counseling or transition time back to civilian life. Less than 48 hours had elapsed from the time I left Saigon as a soldier, to the time I was a civilian on the streets of San Francisco. I was resilient and could handle dramatic changes like this but I understand why many soldiers had trouble making such drastic transitions from a wartime military to a peace time civilian environment. I remember leaving the processing center in civilian clothes with my duffel bag and being aware that there was a lot of anti war sentiment and feeling very strange. I went directly to the San Francisco airport and made flight arrangements to return home to Arizona by flying into Phoenix. My older sister, Betty, met me at the airport in a convertible she had borrowed for the occasion. Her husband, Mike, was an ex Marine so he understood a lot of what I was feeling. After an overnight stay and visit with my sister and her family, I flew back to Flagstaff and re- united with my father, Charlie, and my brother and sister, Chuck and Margaret. I was home!

During my two year military enlistment, I had changed from a semi irresponsible boy to a responsible young man. I realized that I had to control alcohol usage rather than allowing alcohol to control me. I also understood better that all my actions had consequences and I had no one but myself to blame for negative consequences. By seeing death and coming close to it myself, I gained a greater appreciation for life and the beauty and joy of my journey through this life. I lost a special girlfriend while I was overseas and while saddened by that loss, realistically, I was not ready to settle down. I had just resumed my quest to discover myself as a person and to decide how to become an independent adult and what career I wanted to pursue after my college studies were complete.

During the time I was in Vietnam, my all consuming goal was to return to college. I would fantasize and plan my college curriculum while in Vietnam as a pleasant exercise to prepare for my return to civilian life. I was eligible for the G.I. Bill and educational assistance and I used that veteran benefit to complete my undergraduate degree. I finally exhausted the remainder of my education benefits during my graduate studies, eight years after getting out of the Army. The educational benefits I received from the federal government prepared me for a good career and life and I never felt like the federal government owed me a living because of my military service. There are many less fortunate veterans, that need help and I felt like I should not be seeking additional assistance when there were so many veterans with greater needs than myself.

I had always wanted to see the world and for a poor boy like me, the Army jump started my plan to see many countries.

I saw more than I wanted to see of Vietnam plus I toured Japan and much of Europe while in the Army. Rather than satisfying my interest for worldwide travel, it has whetted my appetite to see more of the world and over the years, I have become a world traveler.

I believe that my military experience helped me to become a more aware human being that can better appreciate alternative cultures, lifestyles, and belief systems. I like to think that I am a better citizen of the world because of my experiences.

A valuable lesson I learned that I want to share is my belief that life can offer us many challenges and many of these are beyond our control. The important thing that we can control is our attitude and this determines how we react to life's challenges. A positive attitude is one of the most important attributes that we can have and it should be cultivated. Accordingly, I consider my two year Army experience as a positive growth event in my life and not a couple of years lost out of my life.

In closing, my military experience made me more appreciative of being born an American and having opportunities that so many people in the world do not have. Being Native American, and living on an Indian Reservation poses additional challenges to many of our people but compared to many parts of the world, we Native Americans, here in America today, are fortunate.